Gone Fishin'...

The 50

Best Waters
in
Pennsylvania

Gone Fishin'...

The 50

Best Waters
in
Pennsylvania

By Manny Luftglass

Gone Fishin' Enterprises
PO Box 556, Annandale, New Jersey 08801

Pictured on the cover: *(On the left.)* A typical upper Delaware River shad, taken by Dave Madl. *(In the middle.)* Tom Illar caught this 27 lb. 13 oz. laker and set the State Record in 1996 on board Road Runner Charters out of North East Marine, Lake Erie. *(On the right.)* Park Ranger Dave Bank caught this fat largemouth bass at Promised Land State Park.

Pictured on the back cover: The Commission Area Fisheries Management Areas Map in full color, courtesy of the Pennsylvania Fish and Boat Commission. *(Under map.)* If I stretched my arms out like the real pro's do, this Wallenpaupack chain pickerel would have looked like a huge muskie, right? (Says the author.)

Gone Fishin' ... The 50 Best Waters in Pennsylvania
By Manny Luftglass

© 2000 Emanuel Luftglass

Published By
Gone Fishin' Enterprises
PO Box 556, Annandale, New Jersey 08801

ISBN: 0-9650261-6-7
UPC: 7 9338013579-9

Photo Credits:
The map and some pictures provided by The Pennsylvania Fish and Boat Commission, other pictures provided by the anglers themselves, plus several helpful stores, guides, and professional photographer Vic Attardo, along with personal photos by the author.

Design & Typography:
TeleSet
Somerville, New Jersey

PRINTED IN THE UNITED STATES OF AMERICA

This one is simple, really.
Who else can you dedicate a book about
the best fishing available in the Keystone State
to than to those folks who make it all possible?

Certainly I want to applaud the many private landowners
who allow fishing to be done from their shorelines.
Ditto a big tip of the Gone Fishin' cap
to the countless clubs that exist in Pennsylvania,
like Trout, Unlimited, etc.

But the biggest of all thanks
go to the people at the
Pennsylvania Fish and Boat Commission
who bring superb fishing to every corner of the state.

To all at "Fish and Boat" who helped me with this book,
like Dick Snyder and his eight Area Fisheries Managers,
big time "Attaboys."
Ditto to Executive Director Peter A. Colangelo
and Press Secretary Daniel B. Tredinnick.
My personal thanks too to Marguerite Davidson,
Stocking Coordinator for the ton of material she provided.

Last but not least, to Art Michaels
who is the editor of the fine
PA Angler and Boater Magazine.

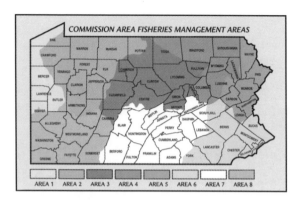

Contents

Peter A. Colangelo
Executive Director

Pennsylvania
Fish and Boat
Commission

Foreword

M ountain streams, tumbling through the forest in a series of cascades and pools...the low grumbling of a bull frog cutting through the morning mist on an otherwise still lake...a cold, clear limestone spring, bubbling through meadows of wild flowers...wooded hills rising from the edge of a meandering river...a golden sunset glistening across the seemingly endless horizon of a Great Lake...Some might call these places paradise. We simply call them Pennsylvania.

"Penn's Woods" were aptly named and even today more than 60% of our state remains forested. Under that canopy lies one of the most abundant and diverse aquatic resources in the nation. From babbling brooks to the wide open expanse of Lake Erie — and everything in between, there's water everywhere in our great state. There are more than 83,000 miles of streams and lakes in Pennsylvania, along with 4,000 inland lakes and ponds covering 160,000 acres. Don't forget to throw in 470,000 acres of Lake Erie either!

But it's not just the quantity of water that makes Pennsylvania an angler's dream; it's the quality. Our state boasts a unique collection of limestone springs teaming with wild trout. The Pocono Mountains are dotted with glacial lakes. The Susquehanna River is widely considered to be the best smallmouth fishing river in the world. At 8,300 acres, Raystown Lake is not only the largest lake entirely in Pennsylvania, it produces new state record striped bass on a regular basis. Teams of American shad surge up the Delaware River each spring. Lake Erie's tributaries fill with feisty steelhead trout each fall. And The Three Rivers area of Pittsburgh is the region's crown jewel. (Note from Manny — two other friends use similar words in discussing their area on following pages. Pennsylvania sure must have a lot of Crown Jewels).

It would be a stretch to say that fishing was invented here in Pennsylvania but we can take credit for much of it's development in America. The first organized fishing club began in colonial Pennsylvania in 1732, the Schuykill Fishing Company. In 1881, the "American Angler," the nation's first fishing magazine was published in Philadelphia. The list of great anglers who called Pennsylvania home reads like roll call at a hall of fame. A section of Spring Creek, near State College, was one of the first demonstration areas set aside to show trout anglers the benefits of aquatic habitat improvement. The results were so successful and the fishing so impressive that to this day the area is known simply as "Fisherman's Paradise."

In addition to the state's naturally reproducing fish populations, the Commission's 14 hatcheries annually stock more than 5 million adult trout and some 100 million warm/coolwater species like muskellunge and striped bass.

Is it any wonder then that anglers take more than 21 million fishing trips here each year? If it sounds like I'm boasting a little, it's simply because there's so much here to be excited about. Much credit for the success of the Commonwealth's fisheries belongs to the men and women of the Pennsylvania Fish and Boat Commission. Founded in 1866, shortly after the Civil War, the Commission is one of the nation's oldest and most effective natural resource agencies. I have often said that this agency's greatest asset is it's people and how they approach their jobs. When you catch a trophy trout that began life in one of our hatcheries, launch your fishing boat from one of our public access sites, or simply call our offices to get information, I hope you'll agree with me.

Equal credit must be given to the nearly 1 million anglers each year who buy a Pennsylvania fishing license. The Pennsylvania Fish and Boat Commission is unlike most government agencies in that we do not receive general fund tax monies to support our programs. Instead, we rely on the sale of fishing licenses and boat registrations to help us meet our mission: "To provide fishing and boating opportunities through the protection and management of aquatic resources." That means that your fishing license is far more than a permit. It is a direct investment in the resource. As you will read about the state's finest fishing destinations, know that you the angler play an important role in preserving that distinction.

In attempting to create a short list of "best fishing spots" in Pennsylvania, this book's author, Manny Luftglass, has taken on a difficult task. What defines a great fishing spot? Is it a waterway where you can catch lots of fish? Or big fish? What about breathtaking views? How about a place to launch your boat? Or do you need shoreline access? Is it easy to get to? Or do you want to get back into the wilderness? What type of fishing do you prefer — sight fishing to rising trout, throwing topwater plugs for bass, trolling for walleye? There are lots of qualities that can make a waterway the "best" choice for you. Fortunately, Pennsylvania has a wide variety of fishing opportunities, including ones to suit your needs. In this book, Manny will introduce you to many of them. Use this book as a guide, but don't forget to do a little exploring on your own. We have waters that are still largely "undiscovered" by anglers. Who knows, you may be gathering material for the next edition of "Gone Fishin'!"

—- **Peter A. Colangelo,** *Executive Director*
Pennsylvania Fish and Boat Commission

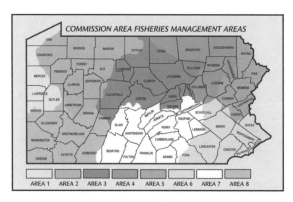

Author's Preface

A s indicated in the dedication, I turned to lots of people for assistance in writing as accurate a book as I could. Besides the many folks at "Fish and Boat" who helped, I also wrote to well over 100 stores in the State who sell fishing licenses, asking them to tell me about their favorite Open to the Public spots. In addition, as Freshwater Field Editor of the New Jersey — Delaware Bay edition of the *Fisherman Magazine,* I also reached out to many stores in the Keystone State who sell the Fisherman to their customers.

I belong to a small but dedicated club, "Carp Anglers Group," which has branches everywhere. Three members — Bill Devine, Bob Miller and John McKean provided details about their own favorite hot spots, for trash fish like bass and pike, as well as their primary game fish — CARP!

Throw in some of my own personal experience in traveling to many of the waters we will discuss and I hope that you both enjoy and learn what you read between the covers of "Gone Fishin' The 50 Best Waters in Pennsylvania."

My goal was to tell you about as many spots as I could with the emphasis on "Open to the Public." In fact, there will only be one site that charges admission — and from the name of the source that gave me details, you may understand — but in no instance did I want to tell you about waters that are truly wonderful and also have "NO TRESPASSING" signs.

I started fishing in 1938 as a three year old and am every bit as enthusiastic about my hobby as I ever was. Hopefully, some of the excitement that I get from fishing and writing about it will rub off onto you! I am "hooked" — how about you?

STOCKING

Just as an example, in the fiscal year 1998-1999, the Commission stocked 5,330,000 adult trout into the various waters of the state! Top that off with another 2,412,323 more little trout and salmon!

On the so-called "warm/cool water" front, they put an incredible number of fish into the waters that year too. While the overwhelming majority were barely visible "fry," another 1,894,331 "fingerling" size were added, and 14,437 "adult" size fish as well.

These fish ranged from true strain to tiger muskellunge, down to the lowly sunfish. From pure to hybrid striped bass to walleye, channel catfish, etc.

The non-trout stockings were of more modestly sized fish because they are easier to transport and stand a good chance of survival in the wild. Put a ten inch trout into a stream and very little exists that will swallow it. On the other hand, a ten inch muskie will be inhaled whole by their far bigger distant cousins they swim over to visit!

So, if you ever wonder what your license money goes towards, the above year's statistics should illustrate it quite clearly. And I didn't just pick "The Best Year" either. In fact, it was simply typical of most years' stockings.

LAWS

Well, I am not about to tell you too much here because no matter what I write, things do change. So let me tell you that the best place to find out what is, and what is not allowed, is the compendium that is published yearly by the Fish and Boat Commission. Called "Pennsylvania Summary of Fishing Regulations and Laws,"

I caught this 3 lb. smallie at Lake Wallenpaupack.

this should be in your tackle box every time you go out!

If you are a "Senior Citizen" who doesn't have to buy a license each year, make sure you pick up a copy of the book anyway from your local tackle store. Since laws do change (like the 2000 reduction in allowable trout bag limits), you really must have this at hand.

It tells you about size and bag limits, open and closed seasons, etc.

For example, in the 2000 Summary, on page 57, a clear definition of what "Year-Round" fishing exists in trout stocked waters as well as an actual list of such places.

Further in that same page is the start of what I guess I could make into a separate chapter of its own (but I will not). From the bottom of page 57 through the end of page 63 I found virtually all the information available about the Public Health Advisories that are in place.

Frankly, I go fishing for the pure fun and enjoyment of catching fish. The last piece of the puzzle sometimes comes from "eating my catch," but honestly, that is not why I love my sport! However, for those of you who do want to take some fish home for a meal, these pages are really quite invaluable and I strongly urge you to read this section of your rule book EVERY YEAR for changes.

As an environmental activist I don't take warnings lightly and I hope you don't either. If you want to be simply a "Catch and Release" guy, that's just fine with me.

SPECIAL REGULATIONS

Again, get that Summary! You will find out about licensing requirements when you fish a bordering state's waters like "The Big D" (Delaware River). Since Pennsylvania anglers often find themselves looking at New York and New Jersey while fishing, the book tells you what to do and not do. Ditto the "Yock," as my friend Bill Devine of Pittsburgh calls the Youghiogheny Reservoir. Here this touches the Keystone State as well as Maryland. Clearly one of my "50 Best" is the Pymatuning Reservoir and here, the book tells you about the rules too since it is also in Ohio.

Some very special regulations are in place regarding bag limits and open seasons for specific bodies of water. Perhaps the most simple one involves striped bass in the Delaware River.

Sexually mature striped bass spawn in the river. Most states, including Pennsylvania, do not allow anglers to keep stripers in January and February. Simply, those that used to be caught in those months were snagged because the waters they were found in were just too cold for active feeding anyway.

The area two part of the Allegheny River produced this fine 'eye.

A striper that meets other rules can be taken in March, but for the next two full months, any "rock" caught from the southerly Pennsylvania state line up to Trenton Falls must be released. Regulators feel (and I agree) that these two months are quite critical. April and May are spawning time.

You may find me talking about the baits I prefer to use wherever I go. Well, the Summary goes into details regarding any special rules that apply to certain waters with some baits. Clearly, "Fly-Only" and "Delayed Harvest Artificial Only" waters must be known. You sure don't want to be found with a five trout limit you were observed catching on salmon eggs when the water being fished has a three fish limit and is "Fly-Only."

I know that it is tempting to catch fish using your own personal logic: "I am going to throw them all back anyway," but that just doesn't work with the badge wearer. Some years' back I fished for lake trout at Heron Lake in New Mexico with a guide. He told me that the best laker bait known to man was live suckers and that was what we used. However, later on, after I caught a beauty, he added that you cannot use suckers for bait at Heron Lake!

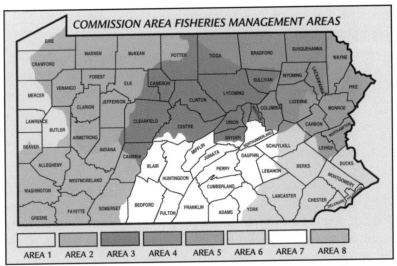

See Key Map on back cover for Area separations in color.

REGIONAL DEFINITIONS

When my main fishing buddy and co-author, Ron Bern and I wrote "Gone Fishin' The 100 Best Spots in New Jersey," and then its' sequel about the top 100 in New York, we tried to figure out how to separate waters and not make our readers completely nuts. We settled on breaking Freshwater and Saltwater apart from each other, and then went into separate sections for rivers, streams, wrecks, and so on.

Well, for Pennsylvania angler wannabies, those who live here or travel to the state and want to catch some fish, I found two different ways to make it lots easier. For one thing, I went for half the spots, because we just don't have an ocean here! We will get into the Delaware's brine, to be sure, but still, I hope you agree that 50 is okay.

There were two different ways to break things apart. One method would have been to talk about all the "best" waters in each of the SIX different law enforcement regions that are located in the state. They are simple to understand — Northwest, Southwest, North-central, South-central, Northeast and Southeast. Honestly, it might have been easier to talk to you about those six sections of the state, but I think I found a better system available to me, and I hope you agree.

Fish and Boat has eight Area Fisheries Managers in the state. Each person has staff to assist and all these folks are true experts, both as to fishing itself, and everything else involved in our hobby. While the six law enforcement groups exist, they also involve items of less interest to anglers.

So I opted to break the state up into the eight different "Areas," one by one, to help you find out where to fish.

Certainly there are "areas" that involve border crossings, like the Delaware and Susquehanna Rivers. In each of the eight group-ings, as pointed out at the start, one of my main sources of help was from the actual area managers, and they assisted greatly in creat-ing my artificial separations.

Therefore, to define the eight areas better, the book will start in area one, which covers Lake Erie, and all or parts of five other counties. Then we swing east to #2 which involves Warren, Forest, Clarion and other places in the vicinity. Five areas in total will be found in the top part of the state, with #5 hitting the upper Delaware, etc. Then we will move down the southeast part of the state into #6 and move westward to #7 and lastly into Area 8 at the southwest section of Pennsylvania.

The actual system I will use will involve alphabetical order per Area. Instead of separating rivers from streams from lakes, etc., we will clump all the hot spots together in an area by the alphabet. In instances that deal with waters that have two or more names, I will show all names at the start of each area, with the names shown on most maps as number one name. Whether the spot is Lake "X" or "X" Lake, you will find it under "X" — for example, in Area One, Lake Erie will be under "E" and Pymatuning Lake under "P."

So, without further delay, let's start "Gone Fishin' The 50 Best Waters in Pennsylvania," okay?

CHAPTER 1

Area One

F isheries Manager Craig Billingsley's part of the state involves all of the Pennsylvania waters of Lake Erie, and the other water found in all or part of five counties in the northwest part of the state.

#1 LAKE ARTHUR

Other than the two big rivers, Delaware and Susquehanna, Lake Arthur seemed to be more popular among my sources than any other body of water in the entire state, and for good reason. Simply put, it holds lots of hungry fish, and after all, isn't that our main goal, to catch fish?

Specific anglers target different species of fish. Found here, among others, are true strain muskellunge, largemouth bass, northern pike, channel catfish, walleye and crappie (in '99, nine year old Steven Frey caught a 17 inch "slab"), lots of yellow perch, and as you will read shortly, some folks concentrate on carp!

To make sure the lake remains excellent, stockings that took place in 1999 included 39,200 more fingerling sized channel catfish, 3,300 true strain muskellunge, 16,100 hybrid stripers, and a whopping 66,000 very small walleye.

Area Fisheries Manager Craig Billingsley wrote to me, advising

*Here's Bob Miller of New Castle resting up for a big carp bite
at the Upper 528 Boat Launch area of Lake Arthur.
(Now is that creature comfort or what?)*

that the waters are stocked annually with walleye, hybrid (my
name, "Rocket") striped bass, and muskellunge. He said that the
lake is best known for muskies and largemouth bass, which are
specially managed under Big Bass regulations.

Several major roads lead directly to Lake Arthur. 79 runs down
near its western shore. Route 422 (Franklin Highway) passes by to
the south. And 528 actually goes over it. Horsepower restriction
boat launch sites can be found in the northwest and southwest corners as well as three just east of 528. At least five other sites can
be found also. The lake is in Moraine State Park.

There are at least 17 specific public access sites to the lake so
you don't have to worry about finding too many "Posted — No
Trespassing" signs here. As stated above, it does have some specific regulations, so make sure you read the Summary of
Regulations before hitting the lake.

Bill Devine of Pittsburgh wrote to tell me that his access is
found off of I-79 North, about an hour above his home. He said that

Muddy Creek (to the east) was dammed many years ago as part of a strip mine reclamation project and Lake Arthur was formed.

Ice fishermen do well on the lake, but in warm water times, channel catfishermen have a ball catching them.

Devine says that Arthur is one of the best and least utilized carp lakes in the state. He likes the Muddy Creek branch area best and reaches it via Route 428 East, off of I-79 and then Route 528 North. While two launch sites are nearby, he prefers the upper one because it is less used. (Well, it WAS less used, until you read this book).

Another "Carper," Bob Miller of New Castle, added to the history lesson Bill Devine gave us. He said that Muddy Creek goes way back to the last great ice age. 1968 was the year that he said the state reformed a dam with modern technology, creating the actual lake.

Lots of fish were stocked originally by the State including walleye, largemouth bass, pike, muskies, crappies, and a variety of baitfish as well as bluegills. Other fish were either added or just popped up unannounced. Hybrid striped bass, plus channel catfish and blue cats were brought to the big lake.

The lake is more than ten miles long and ranges in width from only 200 yards to nearly a full mile wide.

Miller's favorite stomping ground can be found at the upper 528 boat launch area where Bill Devine also fishes. Bob has caught fish ranging from many a yellow perch and sunfish, to carp up to 20 pounds, channel cat's up to 10 pounds, largemouth bass of good size, and northern pike up to three feet long!

When fishing from shore with bait, Bob generally uses a two ounce bell sinker to get distance, with a rubber bead as a buffer between it and his barrel swivel. He prefers smaller live bait, even for the bigger fish like muskies, pike, channels and walleye. Hooks in sizes 1-4 are favored and he often baits with night crawlers.

Little known is the fact that the bigger "Green Giants" like pike and muskies often go after dead bait more than live. A British angler named Tony Broomer taught me to use dead baitfish that float for pike. To insure this, just freeze your leftover live bait in baggies of 10-15 or more fish and as you thaw them out, put a few in your pail. Some will float (air bladders were probably inflated when they died) and others will sink. Those that float make the best dead bait. Think about it — your sinker is on the bottom, and the bait floats up off the bottom to the length of your leader. It flops around looking more like a dying bait than a dead one!

Miller likes to inject smelt with Game Fish Attractant in the cold windy days of March and April for his pike. Either way, don't only use live bait. I catch tons of pike and lake trout on floating alewife herring. A 24 inch walleye went home with me in June of 2000 that took a "popped-up" bait.

Kind of gross to be sure, but Bob likes to target bluegills at times. His style involves getting a cheap can of bread crumbs, squirting them with a few blasts of crappie attractant, and adding water to form a ball. Now comes the gross part. Add 20 or 30 maggots (OPTIONAL) per ball, and throw the whole mess close to where you will fish. If you have maggots, bait with them where you chummed, and you will surely catch a gang of bluegills. If you don't want to go with maggots, bait with small worms and you will do well also.

(If you ever meet me at a Fishing Show, remind me to tell you the story of Maggot Michael of Manchester) — or just pick up a copy of my fourth book, "Gone Fishin' For Carp," and check it out on page 51.

Bass anglers find their typical lures to work well here. Just remember that while the lake is best known for large bucketmouth's, it also has the two mouthful's of teeth we talked about too. Dark rubber worms are always good in the warm water by day and in very early or late times, fish noisy topwater lures. If a large wake occurs though, prepare to fight a "Green Giant" (muskie or pike).

#2 ELK CREEK

The largest of the various streams that feed into Lake Erie, an incredible 250,000 yearling sized steelhead trout were recently stocked in the creek. The idea, of course, is to get the fish to

*Guide Pat McKinstry with a good sized steelie he caught at
Elk Creek in the fall of '99 while using, as he suggests,
a single egg.*

migrate into Erie, grow, and return to the creek to spawn once they reach sexual maturity. Catches over the past few years have indicated that prior stockings have produced some wonderful results.

Fishing Guide Patrick McKinstry of Erie calls Elk "The Crown Jewel of steelhead streams in PA." (Earlier and much later on you will see that other serious anglers use a variation of that name in connection with two other areas)

Pat started to work for the new Gander Mountain Sporting Goods store in Erie in July of 2000, but his real love comes from being out there on the water, fishing and or guiding.

To illustrate how good a fishery exists here, the Jan/Feb 2000 edition of the Pennsylvania Angler & Boater Magazine carries a photo of writer Samuel Shiels and his son holding a foursome of steelies of nice size, and this goes back to a day in 1992. Nine years later, Nick Bohonek of Pittsburgh released a 9½ pounder back into the creek in the fall of 1999.

Top fishing occurs each fall and the steelhead rainbows ("Sea Run" — even though the "Sea" is Lake Erie) are on station and ready to tear drags! Remember though, that the Elk is normally clear and not very fast of current. Rainwater determines the height of the creek but the norm is low water, so techniques need to be adjusted for this. So if you are going after these fish, you need to disguise your presentation as much as possible in order to fool them.

Coho salmon and brown trout are also stocked at Elk Creek to add to the available mixture of salmonoids.

Elk enters Lake Erie a little to the west of State Road 18 in Girard Township. It begins below McKean and the entire range of the creek offers some wonderful fishing.

Springtime means trout. Many recently stocked as well as some sea-runs that make it back into the creek late, or simply ones that winter over. As the water warms up, the salmonoid fishery is just about over because survivors swam back into the cooler waters of the lake. Downstream though, anglers can still catch catfish, panfish and bass.

When the water is very clear, a normal situation, the folks who handle the longest of long rods do the best. Called "Noodle" rods due to their length and flexibility, a Noodle is designed to allow an angler to fish very light line and yet be able to challenge the strength of these somewhat dull colored rainbows.

The longer the rod, the more skill needed by the angler, but if he or she knows the score, a fine score indeed can be marked on the tally list.

Guide McKinstry favors a 9 foot light action stick, those that are traditionally called "Steelhead rods," to assist further in controlling the strong fish. His favorite is a St. Croix Wild River model, but less expensive models are also made by Browning and Berkley.

As autumn starts, fish move from the lake into the lower river and when this begins, the better action remains close to the lake, around the Route 5 Bridge. Once the water really gets cold, the fish migrate way upstream and can be located off I-79 up at McKean.

A good access point for anglers can be found at the mouth of Elk on Route 5, west of Route 18. Just below the mouth, F&B recently built a parking lot on the east side of the creek.

If you are using waders, make sure you keep a hand free to use your walking stick and creepers on your feet aren't a bad idea either. Having invented what I call "The Green Rock Flop," I normally don't try "Walking on Water," but if that is your thing, do it with caution please.

As the river flows southward, and the fishing gets better in colder water, you can park and find steelies off Township Route 543 on both sides of the railroad tracks.

Another good area is at the Route 544 steel bridge. If the current is very light, I suggest you fish the upstream side. But if it is moving fast, you will probably do better on the downstream angle.

Perhaps the most heavily fished place is called "The American Legion Hole," situated off Route 20. The key is to find the American Legion Park and people who don't like to walk a lot fish downstream of it, because if you go up above, you will huff and puff to get back to your car.

Pat McKinstry said that you can do well right under Route I-79 also.

Several other sites exist where you can find some good action, but if you have the time, get to Elk Creek and do some exploring of your own.

Bring your 9 foot 5-7 weight fly rod too, and an assortment of dark flies. While light colored ones work too, normally, the darker the better if you are into fly fishing. A Weldon Mini-eye jig also work well often. Try one in black and white, 1/64 or 1/80 ounce.

Bait fishermen use the same kind of stuff as we use on the Salmon River that goes into Lake Ontario. Of course, they have even more regulations there to deny meat hunters the right to snag king salmon heading upstream.

If bait is your thing, bring a wide variety, as well as several different hook sizes. Remember, if your bait isn't bouncing on the bottom, you won't do too well.

An assortment of floats will help, and keep your sinkers to a minimum weight. Just enough lead to bounce your offering downstream, without getting hung up too often, is just what you will want.

While a variety of eggs, salmon or fresh-skein are often the best, take everything but the kitchen sink with you, just in case. You never know what they will hit. Pat feels that a single FRESH egg on a small hook is tops.

Elk Creek also has a sucker run and the steelies like to gobble fresh sucker roe, so check at your local tackle store to try and get something that matches the spawn. In fact, if you can somehow get a hold of some sucker spawn, try squeezing it into a tin holding a few maribu or small bucktail jigs, allowing the scent to invade the fuzz.

Please do respect the beauty of your surroundings and if you really are into fishing for a sport, don't take any home to give to a friend, instead, practice Catch and Release. Most of the people who say "Sure, bring me some," when you are about to leave home, are either not there when you knock on their door, or worse, complain because you didn't fillet the fish for them!

#3 LAKE ERIE

Pa. Fish and Boat offers not less than 20 public access sites to their section of this truly "Great Lake." They start to the west at Raccoon Park, run by local government. You can launch your high powered boat or fish from shore here. With many stops in between, at the eastern tip of Pennsylvania's shoreline of Lake Erie, you get to North East which allows you to launch at their two double wide ramps and also has a huge Marina with all the amenities.

In fact, I heard from Captain Tim Truitt who works out of the North East Marina, who said that you can find his facility approximately 20 miles east of Erie and 1½ miles west of the New York State border. From I-90, take Route 89 North about 5 miles to Route 5 East and 2½ miles later, you are there!

All kinds of services are available including wet, dry and rack storage, with a full service store. You can rent a boat here or charter one of the knowledgeable skippers to take you out to some exciting action. Top that off with free parking for up to 500 vehicles and you may realize why I started at the east end of the lake in this "Best," instead of over to the western corner.

Tim said that the action generally starts early in April if the ice is gone. Steelhead trout are taken in front of 20 and 16 mile creeks, only two miles from the Marina. Smallmouth "Trophy Season" (READ the Summary, Please) runs from 4/15 though 6/16 and 40 to 50 bronzeback catches daily are quite common. 5-6 pounders are caught on a regular basis.

Come the end of May or early in June, based on water temperature, walleye take hold and Tim suggests fishing for the 'eyes at the "W's" and off Freeport Road — two miles west of the Marina. Summer brings even better walleye action with the fish fattening up on schools of smelt and emerald shiners out in deeper, cooler water.

Want trout? Steelhead and big lake trout are commonly caught out in deeper water with the steelies up and the lakers down. Tim suggests fishing through September at "The Mountain" for trout. It's found north /northwest of his facility, about 4½ miles offshore.

Once the water drops to 55 degrees, the signal is on for inshore fishing with migration inshore starting for spawning steelies, (upwards of 1,000,000 yearling steelies were stocked in 1999 at various points at the lake). And the smallmouth get serious again!

As noted at the top, Lake Erie looks more like an Ocean, and acts like one too. Therefore, if you are launching a small boat, or for that matter, a good-sized craft, make sure you have all the standard life-saving gear. Get an accurate weather report before you sail. Much of the eastern end of the lake is rather shallow, compared with Lake Ontario, which it ultimately dumps into, through the Niagra River and the Welland Canal in New York. Storms tend to create mountainous waves that can turn over some of the biggest boats around. So again, hesitate on the side of caution, and maybe stay on land and take the boat out "Tomorrow."

*This youngster caught this fine walleye on the Walleye Wizard
out of North East Marine Service, Lake Erie.*

Coho ("Silver") and Chinook ("King") salmon swim in the lake, but they have not taken hold as well as those in Lake Ontario. The state continues to try to make a Coho fishery farm though, stocking 137,000 yearling Coho's into four of Erie's tributaries. Some beauties are caught, both off-shore, and again, once they start their one-way spawning swim into the creeks they were stocked at when very small. Try trolling for them and steelhead with NK28 spoons in September and October, right in front of the creek mouths.

The "Trenches" can be found on the western end of the state's waters of Lake Erie. Try heading five miles out from the Walnut Creek Access area to reach the first trench which your depth finder will clearly point out by a change of reading of at least 10 feet. The action here can be wonderful while pulling spoons.

A wide variety of fish can be found in the lake. Kids love to catch fish, and size is not as important to them as is the action itself.

Yellow perch, perhaps the fish caught in greatest numbers in Lake Erie, are very popular, but don't forsake the huge population of red-eyed rock bass. Neither fights very well, but once the baby night crawler is inhaled and the bobber goes down, your youngster will squeal with delight and better yet, a meal of fresh perch and rock bass cannot be beaten.

Walleye are among the most popular fish in the lake, but small-mouth anglers will fight you and probably prove that their favorite is number one. For walleye, some guys go out in the coldest of nights each spring and cast from shore. Live bait is best because the fish are close in, looking for little steelheads to move out of the streams. A large emerald shiner may be a little difficult to keep alive, but they do make some of the best bait around for 'eye's'. In addition, a big night crawler will always produce results.

The wonderful world of the "Net" brought me to 'Fish Erie,' which gave me lots of useful data about the lake. It had a separate section on Presque Isle Bay, which is situated right in the middle of the Pennsylvania waters of Lake Erie. As many as ten public access sites are situated around the shoreline of Presque Isle Bay, so here may be the place you want to try if your time is limited.

Pat McKinstry holding a typical night time channel cat at
Presque Isle, Lake Erie.

Looking at a map or Atlas, you will see that the area is easily reached from the City of Erie, and that more safe "lee" can be found here than anywhere else nearby because Presque Island itself blocks much of all but the strongest of a variety of winds. It's waters are relatively shallow too.

If it is really ugly outside, and you don't want to fish from shore, you can always take a trip to the Flagship Niagra or drive out to Presque Isle Peninsula State Park via Route 832. In fact, I counted seven boat launch sites which are on or leading to the island. We spoke earlier about guide Pat McKinstry. He added that the park has several miles of beaches, a bike path, many miles of hiking trails, and plenty of access for persons with disabilities.

Besides the other fish discussed so far, Area Manager Craig Billingsley points out that netting samples taken at Presque Isle Bay in 1998 showed lots of 25-26 inch northern pike and some better than three feet long. He adds that hardly an angler targets these fish here, so add them to your "Shopping List." (By the way, when fishing for pike with bait, you will get cut off once every five to ten bites if you don't use a wire leader, but I have found that I get so many more hits without wire, that it is worth catching more than getting less action). If a really, really big "Green Giant" appears at the end of your line, it could also be one of the many muskellunge known to roam the lake.

Bait fishermen who are after smallmouth bass swear that the only bait to use is crawfish. Called "Crabs" on Lake Ontario, it is true that craw/crayfish are dynamite bait. I have caught many a bronzeback while fishing suspended below a three inch slider float. Simply find the bottom and rig the float so that your bait will dangle a short distance above the bottom. If you let the "Crab" sit, it will find a hole and hide, so it is far better to barely nudge the bottom at most. Just look for bottom depth changes on your scope and if it is a good machine, you will also see rubble below. A flat, open bottom is not the place to fish.

McKinstry says that, in the spring, Presque Isle Bay offers the "Best smallmouth fishery in the planet!" He likes to use Gitzit tube jigs for them, and added that many a shore-based angler does well from the north and south piers using crayfish.

Some folks catch more smallies on jigs than bait but whatever you use, treat them with respect, they deserve it.

Several weird species of fish are in Lake Erie too. Most are protected, but just as a point of interest, let me tell you that it has sturgeon, gar and sea lamprey eels. You can have all the lamprey I catch, by the way. Having caught several trout that had lamprey suction holes on their bodies, I sure don't want to touch one. I can even remember seeing spawning lampreys hanging onto rocks on a waterfall at the Raritan River in New Jersey. Yuck! The lake also holds bowfin, called "Dogfish" in Canada. I caught a 5 pounder once on a live frog and what I thought was a beauty of a largemouth turned out to be this ugly critter.

Don't forget the largemouth bass population at Presque Isle too, by the way. Spring electro-fishing in the bay in 1999 found a bunch of good sized bass in 3-8 foot weed beds in the Marina Lake section.

Here's a few more tips from our guide friend, Pat — in the fall, anglers catch lots of perch from the north and south piers, and come winter, go with smelt or minnows for burbot. He calls them the best tasting fish on the lake!

Still more — tons of big channel catfish are caught using heavy rods while casting from shore with fresh store shrimp for bait. Pat uses a one ounce egg sinker stopped by a barrel swivel with a one foot leader below and a size one wide gap hook at the business end.

Try creek mouths for the channel's like Trout Run, Elk, Walnut and 8 Mile. Fish from dusk to shortly after midnight, or from 4-5 in the morning. Bring a lantern!

If you listen to John McKean of my club, "Carp Anglers Group," you will also note that he finds carp in the Presque Isle section of the lake, so add that to your list of available fish.

Enjoy the lake with the 11th largest surface area in the world!

#4 PYMATUNING RESERVOIR

Located in Crawford County, Area Fisheries Manager Craig Billingsley calls this one of the two top lakes in his entire district. He points out that the lake receives annual stockings of both walleye and muskellunge and year round rules here are less strict than throughout most of the State for those anglers who like to take fish home for a meal. For example, the 2000 summary showed that walleye and walleye hybrids can be kept 365 days per year, with a 15 inch size limit, and a bag total of six. Muskies and muskie hybrids are also "keepers" the whole year and two can be taken if they reach 30 inches. We are NOT suggesting taking any home, but we're simply pointing out what the law is here.

Spring samplings conducted via trap netting in 1999 were very promising. Walleye in huge numbers and impressive size were found in 61 net sets. A little less than 2,000 walleyes were found and more than half were 15 inches or better. A fat female weighed more than 10 pounds.

Muskie samplings too, that spring, were very good. 81 were netted and nearly all reached or exceeded the 30 inch size limit. The largest went nearly 4 feet long!

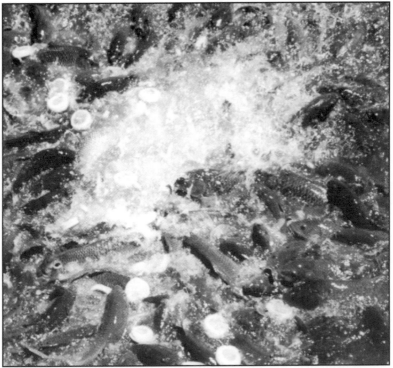

*"Got Bread?" Pittsburgh's Bill Devine sent us this photo of carp
going nuts after stale bread at the Pymatuning Spillway.*

Walleye exceeded the nettings made in 1998 more than a year
later. And the 'lunge numbers were more than double the best rate
than in the previous seven years.

The "Atlas" shows that Pymatuning also holds crappie, largemouth bass, and white bass. By the way, if you cross a male white
bass with a female striped bass, you get the craziest beast around,
called "hybrid"— more on 'em later.

You can find two launch sites (limited horsepower) a bit south of
Route 8 on the northern part of the lake.

What else is in Pymatuning? Well, Craig Billingsley suggests
fishing the north end if you want the biggest bluegills on his beat.
He also likes the lake for channel catfish. The 1/2/2000 edition of
'Pa. Angler and Boater' has a picture of Smilin' Kevin Marsh, age

10, holding a 4¾ pounder.

"Carpers" like Bill Devine favor the spillway where tourists come to throw bread and watch ducks walking on the backs of countless numbers of carp that are feeding on the stale loaves. I've seen similar sites in Hershey Park, Pa., and at Lake Mead. Bill said Pymatuning, in his opinion, may be the world's number one carp fishing spot!

Note too that the lake is also over the state line into Ohio, so watch out for the special regulations that exist there.

#5 SHENANGO RIVER LAKE

The north west part is more river than lake, but as it flows to the southeast, this water slows down to a lake. Found in Mercer County, three boat launches that don't restrict horsepower can be found here, and you can moor overnight.

Known to contain both large and smallmouth bass, caught at Shenango are also northern pike, true muskies, walleye and lots of panfish.

Area One Manager Craig Billingsley told us that the lake has some really nice channel catfish and you can also find hybrid bass here. He points out that 1996-1999 walleye findings were all good and he expects fine fishing for them.

1999 stockings included 3,300 fingerling true strain muskies, 17,800 hybrid bass, plus walleyes into the lake. The river section got still more walleyes (19,000 little ones), along with channel catfish and 800 fingerling tiger muskellunge.

Several roads cross right over the lake including Route 846 to the north, and Route 18, southeast of Pymatuning Station.

Nine public access sites can be found at Shenango with shore fishing available at each location.

A Big Bass Program with special regulations pointed out in the Summary exists here.

In a Spring, 1999 sampling, the State electro-fished and found 120 largemouth bass as well as 75 smallies in three evenings. The longest "bucket" was nearly 20 inches and the best smallmouth was almost 16 inches long.

#6 WALNUT CREEK

The state puts lots of steelheads into this, the second most popular creek that runs into Lake Erie. As with Elk Creek, a quarter of a million small steelheads were stocked into Walnut Creek in 2000!!

A team effort of Fish and Boat combined with the Pennsylvania Steelhead Association and several other groups and agencies, took place in 1999 to create "natural" fish holding holes. These big pools, that didn't exist until the bulldozers built them, are really working well. Fish that reach as big as 10 pounds are not at all uncommon now.

You can find Walnut Creek's beginning east of Exit 41, off I-79. The run to the lake goes through Manchester and later, in cold water, as far upstream as the Millcreek Mall.

A marina can be found right at the mouth of the lake and this is where the steelies first start biting each fall.

The "Walnut Creek Access Area" run by the state, is located here with all sorts of services that can be found until it shuts down in November when it really starts to get cold. It's west of Erie International Airport and can be found off Route 5, at the Manchester Road Soccer Field.

The "Manchester Hole" is one of the "Natural" holes created by man that we discuss at the start of this section. It can be mobbed when the run is really on and no parking signs will make you a bit upset. Aside from such displeasure, the pool is south of the Manchester/Dutch Road Bridge and the access spot for legal entry is on the west side of the creek.

Another good area is at the Walnut Creek Gun Club, which is located on Route 20, between Manchester and Dutch Road.
Also try at the Millcreek Mall for yet more access.

Several other locations are on Walnut Creek, but remember, it is heavily fished in the fall, so try to pick a mid-week period to avoid the biggest crowds.

Walnut is fished with bait more than flies and that is simply because there is not enough water for a wader to chase up and downstream without banging into another guy.

Here, as with Elk Creek, a Steelhead or Noodle Rod works best to help fight a big steelie, and remember, bait is generally more productive. Go with salmon eggs, but if you can get some really fresh spawn skein (like out of a steelhead that a nice neighbor just caught and cleaned), try it, they'll like it!

Carry some fine mesh to wrap it in, but if it is very fresh, you will probably be able to wrap your line around the mess and hang enough of a hold on the bait to present it to a fish without containment. Pat McKinstrey favors white, blue and pink if he has to go with netting. As on Elk Creek, he still prefers a single fresh salmon egg.

Make sure to bring some baby night crawlers for when the water is a bit high and dark. Maggots, two or three to a little hook, bouncing bottom, will also create action.

My biggest river steelie ever hit the most un-natural kind of bait; unless you think it out, and then it may make sense to you. Instead of a dark salmon egg, or dark Power Bait, I was using a miniature orange marshmallow. This "bait" bouncing and still floating downstream got inhaled by a 10 pounder and I can still feel the fight!

As for an Honorable Mention; Another site that comes to mind is Neshannock Creek. It offers huge northern pike.

CHAPTER 2

Area Two

A world of data was provided to us about this part of the state, by Area Fisheries Manager, Ronald D. Lee. Area two encompasses the eastern sides of Erie and Crawford Counties, as well as all or some of ten other counties. So, Mr. Lee certainly has a large part of the state to cover. His technician Al Woomer also provided some dynamite assistance to me.

#7 ALLEGHENY RESERVOIR

Very long and narrow, the reservoir starts as a river in New York, and runs through much of Warren County, Pa., where it splits back into the river again to the southwest, and then dumps into another hot spot, Kinzua to the southeast.

Two boat launch sites exist way up at the northern tip of Warren County, one at the end of Onoville Road and the other in Willow Bay. Within the reservoir proper, you can find another one about half-way down on the western shore. Lastly, you can also put your boat in just above the eastern side of the Complanter Bridge.

The Allegheny Reservoir boasts large quantities of bass, both large and smallmouth. True strain muskellunge and their smaller cousins, northern pike, can be caught too. Does it have walleye's? Well, how about the 1999 stocking of THREE MILLION that took place? Of course the overwhelming majority of these "fry" sized babies probably never saw life a few days after they were stocked, because of naturally caused death, along with having been eaten by many a hungry critter. Just think though, what an effort, and hopefully with some return of consequence in the future.

100,000 fingerling sized channel catfish were put into the reservoir in 1999, and many of these will probably make it because they have the ability to survive in the worst of conditions. Chances are they averaged four inches or so in length and while many have already been consumed, you can bet that thousands will be on station in good size for years to come.

In total, not less than 25 different species of fish are in Allegheny, ranging in alphabetical order from black crappie to yellow perch.

Mr. Lee pointed out that 50 public access points exist on the lake with 29 of them within a short walk from a public road. In the fall of 1997, the state figured that as many as 1800 cars and 414 trailers can actually be parked around its shore. By the way, 99% of the shoreline is fishable, making for very friendly conditions.

335 boats can be moored at the various facilities and while I told you above about four ramps, Mr. Lee said that actually nine ramps exist!

A 55 foot high dam (Kinzua) contains the water and it was built in 1966. This dam actually created the reservoir by holding up the flow of the Allegheny River and allowing it to move in a more controlled manner southward.

Owned by the Army Corps of Engineers, its 12,000 acres boasts the State Record (as of the Spring of 2000) on walleye's and northern pike. Back in 1984, a 53.14 pound muskellunge was caught and that was only 5 ounces lighter than the state record muskie caught way back in 1924 in Conneaut Lake.

Super catches of smallmouth bass are made in the lake, and as already discussed, count on it being wonderful for walleye. Because it has lots of cold water running through it, with all the oxygen needed, the lake has a fine population of brown trout with fish being netted annually by the state that reach 29 inches. Now you know that a 29 inch brownie is a beast — no doubt weighing 10 to 12 pounds.

White bass, the fish generally found in the southern portions of the country, are here in very large numbers. They do not reach much weight but are very fine fighters. When you mix the milt of a male white bass with the roe of a female striped bass, you get my crazy hybrid, Rocket!

Bluegills, crappie and yellow perch please the little ones too, but the lake is far better known as a producer of monster-sized fish, even including huge carp.

#8 ALLEGHENY RIVER (PARTIAL)

The Allegheny River starts in Potter County, going through McKean County, and it then enters New York, returning back to Pennsylvania later. It travels through Warren County, all in Area 2, all the way down to Lock and Dam 6 in Armstrong County. We will talk about its southern section later on in Area 8.

The river offers a very good brown trout action up top, and brownies are taken down to the vicinity of Port Allegheny in McKean County. Ron Lee told us that it is here where the water warms up a bit and more traditional coolwater fishing joins with the coldwater trout.

Walleye, muskie and smallmouth bass are the main targets in the river, but don't forsake the large numbers of northern pike it holds. The River leaves the State north of Eldred, Pa., and as noted in the previous "Best" site, it re-enters at the Allegheny Reservoir. Down below, as it discharges through the Kinzua Dam, water temperatures seldom exceed 70 degrees. Therefore, even though the river holds warmwater fish, it also can support trout from the dam down to the mouth of Conewango Creek near Warren, Pa., a seven mile section. An angler caught two brownies in excess of 30 inches in March, 1998, at the mouth of the Creek! Another angler had three keeper sized muskellunge one day that February below the mouth of the Creek.

A ¾ mile run from the Dam to Dixon Island offers adequate parking, toilets, and a small boat launch ramp on the south bank

Technician Al Woomer sent us this picture of a big flathead catfish caught in the area 2 part of the Allegheny River.

adjacent to Route 59. You can park and fish during the day from shore for big brown trout on the north bank at the Allegheny National Fish Hatchery.

Really good catches occur just below the dam and by far, anything that duplicates the appearance of the emerald shiners that brown trout like to eat will work well. Mid-range and size stickbaits will do the trick, but the fly guys produce fine catches with large streamers. Try to use a fly that has mylar mixed in to give off the glisten you find in emerald shiners. Yet another preferred natural bait is crawfish. A big wooly bugger is another idea for fly folks.

Special regulations are in place regarding this stretch so, as pointed out often already, check out that Summary! At the writing of this book, the reg's called for two trout per day maximum with a 14 inch minimum size limit.

The big three — smallies, 'eye and muskellunge, are found in excellent quantity in this seven mile area, with the trout.

Once again, as we head down river, the same three are present throughout the free flowing water, as well as the lock and dam sections below. At the Tidioute/Tionesta area, flathead catfish are caught each summer. Very few anglers go after them even though they have been caught in excess of 20 pounds. Fish for them at night in the bigger rocky bottom pools down to the lock and dam pools.

The dams offer a tremendous sauger fishery each spring. If you want action, a sucker run occurs in the spring too. I took a 4+ pounder on a baby night crawler in the spring of 2000 and for a moment, thought I had a monster! As with many of the waters found in Pennsylvania, you can catch lots and lots of carp in the Allegheny River. Having been raised fighting the current, a ten pound "Big-Scaler" will tear up the drag on cheap reels so make sure you go after them with good, smooth running reels.

Stocking records for 1999 showed that a wide variety of fish were put into the river. In McKean County, it got muskellunge and walleye. Ditto Warren and Venango Counties. Armstrong County received both along with tiger muskies, and even paddlefish! In 1998, 150,000 brown and rainbow trout were stocked from the Kinzua Dam down to Conewango Creek.

#9 CLARION RIVER LAKE, EAST BRANCH

Found in Elk County partially in Elk State Park, the lake is on the headwaters of the East Branch of the Clarion River itself, upstream from Johnsonburg. It was created in 1952 with construction of the 56 meter high dam.

Boat launches can be reached up at the northern section as well as way down to its southern tip above the east branch dam. There is no speed limit, but please exercise caution and respect. The two sites can accommodate 110 cars with as many as 80 trailers. Ice fishing is allowed under safe conditions.

A variety of fish are caught in the lake including trout, tiger muskellunge, walleye, bullheads and an assortment of panfish.

Yearling lake trout were stocked in 1999, and you can count on these slow growing fish reaching considerable size as they feed on the wide variety of small fish.

I catch more lakers on bottom in deep water, on what I call my "Uncle Nick" method than any other way. In brief, this involves a ¾ ounce sinker, stopped by a dark barrel swivel, with three feet of your own reel's mono-below, and at the business end, a number 3906 size 6 MUSTAD hook. A large golden shiner is the bait, but the style is kind of weird.

Drop the whole deal down below your double — anchored boat and let the sinker sit on the bottom with a few inches of slack. Your bait will raise up and swim on the 3 foot "leash," and any lakers nearby will be able to spot them. It works!

As with other waters, the two story lake had Acid Mine Drainage problems, but significant reductions occurred in the '70's and since that time, the fishing has improved greatly.

If you are looking for a site that offers the ultimate in beauty, try this spot. A few homes can be seen up-ridge of the lake, but otherwise, the shoreline is completely clear of development. New Jersey Anglers can close their eyes and picture what Lake Hopatcong looks like — the biggest lake in the Garden State, and then smile when they think of what the second biggest spot is, Round Valley Reservoir.

Hopatcong, home to wonderful fishing, is also literally ringed with homes, marinas, etc. The "Valley" has nothing but trees!

Several streams that feed into the lake are well stocked with trout and a few even contain excellent wild trout populations, so whatever you are after, they can be found.

#10 CLARION RIVER, incl. E. & W. BRANCHES

Trout lovers, take note! This is the spot to try!

Another of the "Best" spots we will discuss was called to our attention by Area Manager Ron Lee.

The Clarion River is formed by its East and West Branches.

The East Branch drains East Branch Lake and offers good holdover trout action, as well as more traditional put 'n take catches augmented by adequate stockings.

Besides the "stockies," the cool water discharged throughout the summer allows for trout to survive and flourish. Wild trout are in the main body and the West Branch but they will certainly be found in the East Branch too.

A 1.15 mile stretch can be found immediately downstream from the East Branch Dam where special regulations exist. This is artificial lure only water so remember to leave the bait in the car!

Trout are stocked in the East Branch, downstream to the vicinity of Indian Run, a stream found near Johnsonburg.

The West Branch produces both brook and brown trout naturally, with the "Wild Brookies" restricted to the headwaters. 18-20 inch brown trout are common in the bigger holes. A short stretch is fly only, which should make those who love the long wand very happy.

Once you reach the main stem of the river at its confluence, still more trout are taken in the vicinity of Cooksburg. At Cooksburg, the river is taken over by smallmouth bass.

Bronzebacks became the dominant fish here due to the slack water created by Piney Dam.

Wild and tame trout, and then smallies — yes!

#11 CONNEAUT LAKE

Our friend John McKean of Glenshaw first told us about Conneaut Lake. He said that it is famed for its sizable populations of both muskies and smallmouths.

It's in Southern Crawford County, below Summit, with northern access via Gehrton Road / #3014 near which a boat launch can be found. You may also reach the southern tip of the lake by way of Route 6 near Sadsbury.

In addition to 'lunge and smallies, the lake holds northern pike, largemouth bass and panfish.

It was "sweetened" in 1999 with stockings of still more muskies, along with walleye fry and yellow perch fingerlings.

Sorry that we don't have too much more to tell you about the lake, but the important thing for you to know is that it has a good population of all the fish noted, so why don't you try it out?

Dan Maltese with a walleye he hit at the west end of Conneaut Lake.

#12 EDINBORO LAKE

Here's another of Area 2's "Best," with little information, I regret, to assist.

The Lake is found in the southern part of Erie County, just above the Crawford County line. Below Washington, its eastern shore is close by Route 99.

Although not very large, separate boat launches are on the east and west shores of the lake and they do not restrict horsepower.

Fry and fingerling sized walleye were stocked in 1999, as well as true strain muskellunge.

The tail end of the 90's saw very good action for walleye's which, of course, prefer dark of day times to others once the air gets warm.

Here's a tip for you bait lovers. Rig a "Slider" float ("Slip Bobber"), to hold your live bait twenty feet down. Cast out away from the boat, open the drag, close your bale, and sit the rod down and wait. Now take some dead bait, and cut them up for chum. Yes, you Philadelphia area anglers who head down to the Jersey shore to fish for bluefish, you know what I mean about "Chum," but throwing some hunks of dead bait out to where your float sits will often get the walleye nuts.

I caught a two pounder in 1999 which I saw throw up not less than a half-dozen pieces of the chum that I had been launching out — and besides, it is good practice for you, just in case "marbles" ever become popular again.

#13 TIONESTA LAKE

The middle of Area 2 houses Tionesta Lake in Forest County.

While Tamarack Lake in the southern part of Crawford County (as you will read soon) may one day replace Tionesta on my list of "Bests" in Area 2, as you will read, Tamarack needs time.

Therefore let's move into the northwest tip of Forest County, at the lower end of the Allegheny National Forest. We will find an outfall of the Allegheny River at Tionesta Dam and this is the beginning of Tionesta Lake. A boat ramp can be found here which doesn't limit speed. Another such ramp is at the lakes' southeast tip, near its joint with Tionesta Creek, at the town of Nebraska off Route 3004, Nebraska Road.

Muskellunge are the main target but the lake also contains smallies and panfish. Fingerling sized muskies were stocked in both the lake and creek. A sizable stocking of fingerling sized (as opposed to teeny little fry) walleye were also put into Tionesta Lake.

The lake contains 480 acres and a biologists survey in April of 2000 showed poor findings of walleye which were stocked from 1995 through 1999. Regrettably, it appeared as if the fish wouldn't stay put, apparently leaving the lake in low level periods during surface water releases. At least, as of that survey, walleye stocking will cease. However, if the fish do show up in later surveys, count on the process being reconsidered.

Smallmouth bass are caught in both good numbers and considerable size. A 22 inch smallie was netted at night during a survey

Three Area 2 Fish and Boat guys electrofishing at Lake Wilhelm.

and that fish probably reached 5 or more pounds. Muskies were also found with a 41 incher being the longest.

Channel catfish are both big and healthy here. Many two-foot and bigger channel's are in the lake. For them, we recommend using chicken liver hunks fished on bottom. Channel catfish will eat just about anything that doesn't try to eat them (like muskies) but a gob of chicken liver cannot be beaten.

Rockbass are a target of pan fishermen, and in the spring, trout leave streams in the Tionesta Creek drainage and are caught in the lake. Brook trout as well as brownies were both netted by the state, and caught by anglers. This site is at the southeast tip of the lake.

#14 LAKE WILHELM

At the alphabetical bottom of Area 2, but hardly at the tail end of my list of the "Best" waters, is Lake Wilhelm. In fact, it is way up on the "Best" list for the whole state.

Find Maurice K. Goddard State Park in Mercer County and you

will get to Lake Wilhelm. Route 79 goes right through it from Williams Corners to Schofeld Corners.

Five boat launch sites are on the lake and, frankly, I love the idea that the lake limits the horsepower you can use. I try to avoid the unlimited waters and fish places like this to avoid the huge waves that big motors can cause.

Ron Lee selected the lake because of its quality of fishing available for largemouth bass, muskies, walleye, bullheads, panfish and carp.

He reported 10 public access sites, with parking for 670 cars and 281 trailers. 80% of the shoreline is open to the public. Ice fishing is both allowed and very good, especially for panfish while using a small jig and mousee.

The main baitfish is the standard golden shiner. In all, 14 species of fish are in the lake, Northern pike included.

If you want a shot at a muskellunge, the best method involves trolling a very large non-jointed plug. The longer the better and because so many crappie and bluegill are in the lake, go with a lure that tries to match the shape of these critters. The more traditional long plug should be replaced by one that is fatter and flatter. Pike will go after the same plug and you can also get surprised from time to time by big bucketmouth bass. A plug that duplicates the broad appearance of a golden shiner ("roach") works too.

Both walleye and true strain muskies were stocked in 1999 to join those already swimming in the lake (and maybe to unintentionally feed some of them also).

Largemouth bass are in Wilhelm in both excellent numbers and quality. It is, far and away, the number one game fish in the lake. Good numbers of 20 inch bass are available.

For muskie anglers, lots of 40 inch fish are caught and Mr. Lee said that 50 inchers are highly likely.

Trophy sized walleye are in the lake, but quality of the fishery fluctuates as a result of inconsistent year class recruitment.

Pan fishermen love Wilhelm because it is chock filled with both black and white crappie. Slab-sized "calico's" are here, and bluegill seem to always be both abundant and big. Yellow perch are also found with brown bullhead and carp.

Friedl's Hunting and Fishing said that this was their favorite panfish lake in the whole state. They liked it for pike, muskies, catfish and bass, yes, but a mess of bluegills that were bigger 'n your hand were found too.

Carp lover John McKean wrote to tell me that maybe the biggest carp around swim in Lake Wilhelm.

Honorable Mention: Well, we told you that Tionesta may be replaced on my "50 Best" list one day by Tamarack Lake. A complete drawdown took place in early 1999 on this Meadville, Crawford County impoundment. The 562 acre lake had to be drained to allow the Commission to make necessary repairs to the dam. An incredible volume of fish of all sizes were removed, and transferred elsewhere, including muskies up to 51 inches and some 8-9 pound walleye.

By June of 2001, a fishing pier will be in place on the Cochranton end, and it will even be wheelchair accessible. The lake was just about full, and it was stocked with 100,000 fathead minnows, plus fingerling largemouth bass and muskies. So, Tamarack? Later, we hope.

Another site that's worth thinking about is Crooked Creek Lake in Armstrong County. Found here are lots of channel catfish, white crappie, plus tiger muskies and largemouth bass.

CHAPTER 3

Area Three

M uch of the center of the State is situated in Area 3. Starting at the very northeast tip of Potter County, it wanders through all or chunks of 15 Counties, making for a lot of area to cover for Fisheries Manager Bruce Hollander. While a wide variety of fish can be found in this, the drainage of the West Branch of the Susquehanna River, the primary target in this area for local anglers, is trout!

Just as an example, for the waters of Clinton County alone, 58,650 trout were stocked in its various moving bodies of water. East of Clinton County, in Lycoming County, yet another 159,600 more trout were stocked. So, if you want trout, think Area 3!

#15 FISHING CREEK

We'll start off at Fishing Creek (is that ever a great name or what?). It, and Little Fishing Creek, ramble around through many towns in Clinton County and part of Centre County.

Trout are the main attraction throughout the Creek, but the lower end, in Lock Haven, has smallmouth bass too.

If you are looking for smallies here, try a number 3 (or 2, if the current is light) silver Mepps spinner with no fuzz. Of course, a pickerel or trout might take hold instead, but this lure is dynamite

Brown trout like this beauty are often caught in Fishing Creek.

for moving water bronzebacks.

If casting from shore, don't make the mistake so many others do and target your casts in a downstream path.

Place your cast straight ahead, or even a few degrees upstream. For example, if casting to water that flows from left to right, drop the lure in at around 11 o'clock on your watch and as it falls, once it reaches 2-3 o'clock and makes it down to bottom, as the spinner starts its rise up, that is when most smallmouth bass or trout will strike!

Within its' waters in Clinton County alone, 2,500 trout were stocked in pre-season in the year 2000, and that doesn't even count the in-season stockings which surely added at least as many more.

An article in the April, 1996 edition of 'Outdoor Life' pointed out that Fishing Creek is a typical limestone creek, which provides adequate nutrients to grow all the aquatic insects needed by trout to survive.

If you are looking for the best year-round flies to try, use tan Caddis in sizes 14 or 16, or the various terrestrials like ants (#16, for example), or big crickets.

Abbreviated as "G. R. H. E." by many, number one nymph of quite a few anglers is the Gold-Ribbed Hare's Ear.

Brookies and brown trout are both stocked and native in the creek. Many are just "stockies," but some reproduce too.

Look for some of your best and biggest trout catches to come from the five-mile special regulation section, The Narrows, which goes through state forest land. Watch out for the green rocks though, one slip could ruin your whole day!

The area from Cedar Springs on down gets heavy stockings of trout, so if you are into "Put 'n Take" fishing, and want to bring some home for dinner, try the part that goes through Mill Hall near Route 64.

#16 GLENDALE LAKE

Thank Area Manager Bruce Hollender for much of the help you will get about this lovely 1600 acre lake.

Glendale is in Cambria County, approximately 20 miles north of Altoona. It reaches maximum depths of 43 feet and was formed by impounding Beaverdam Run, Mud Lick, Killbuck Run, and Slate Lick back in 1962. It takes a lot of pounding by fishermen, but it still pleases most who fish it.

The northernmost tip is off State Road 1021, at the town of Glendale, thus the name. State Road 1027 hits its southern end.

A 10 h.p. maximum exists here so you folks who like to fish a car-topper can do so with more safety since the mountain-sized waves the big guys throw will not be found.

Bruce told me that you can find northern pike and their big cousins, muskellunge, along with the smallest clan member, pickerel, plus largemouth bass and walleye in the lake. Also present are bowfin and a wide variety of panfish, with bluegill, black crappie and yellow perch the primary "pan" residents, followed by bullhead, pumpkinseed and rockbass.

Mr. Hollander also said that the smaller, shallow and weedy part of the lake at Slate Lick contains lots of carp.

The Atlas also said that tiger muskies are here, so if correct, that brings the mouthful of teeth clan members to four in total, with pickerel, pike and true-strain's.

If you want further details about Glendale, call Prince Gallitzin State Park at 1-814-674-1000. The park surrounds the lake and offers "extensive and outstanding" facilities.

The lake has very little bottom structure but inshore, the weed beds are substantial and this is where you should look for the "Green Giants." It contains a long and irregular shoreline, which is well wooded, and many bays are here as well.

#17 SAYERS LAKE

There are at least three towns called Howard in the state, so if you are looking for Sayers Lake, check out the town in Centre County called Howard and you will find the lake.

Area Manager Hollander feels that this lake, in the southern part of his section, is just the ticket for warm water anglers. I hope you will agree.

Look for the lake off of Route 150 which travels near its western side. Route 26 goes across it too at its southern juncture with Foster Joseph.

Sayers Lake is quite long, running from southeast to northwest, and covers 1730 acres. It wraps itself around Bald Eagle State Park which is itself a lovely place to check out. Seven boat launches are right in the park, as well as a nice marina.

For even more help locating it, head about 25 — 30 miles southwest from State College in Centre County, or just find Ridge Crest Road off of Route 150, and you will reach the northern tip of the lake.

Horsepower restrictions do not exist here, so exercise caution if you are in a small boat. While most anglers will slow down when nearing an anchored rig or a johnboat, the speed merchants often don't have a clue what havoc they wreak.

A dam was built in 1969 by the Army Corps of Engineers to help with flood control, and the lake resulted. They draw it down each autumn for flood storage and then bring it back up to full pool late the next spring.

The deepest part of Sayers can be found near the dam, at 68

feet. Despite its fertility, aquatic vegetation is limited here and major fish habitat is provided by ripraps along its causeways and levees. Stone and gravel bars from old railroad and road beds offer fine homes too. There are rocks and cattails along the shoreline so, all in all, Sayers is a lake that many a predator can find a hiding place in.

The main predators are largemouth and smallmouth bass. The rocky area, of course, are where you can find ample populations of smallies. Tiger muskellunge are stocked, and so too are channel catfish with 8,650 cat's being put in in 1999 alone.

A fine panfish lake, Sayers is one of the 1999 Enhanced Special Regulation waters, which places a 7 inch minimum size limit on sunfish (pumpkin and bluegills) with a 20 fish (combined species) bag limit, and a 9 inch minimum size and 20 fish creel limit on crappies.

The bobber kids enjoy super catches of yellow perch with the crappie, but Sayers also has bluegill, pumpkinseed and brown bullheads. Just bait up with a meal worm and have the bucket ready. However, if your perch or sunny starts to get very, very heavy, that could just be a tiger muskie that ate it at the other end of your line.

I have never met Mr. Hollander, but I like him anyway — because of his great respect shown to carp. He told us that Sayers Lake has a sizable population of "Mr. Man" too.

If you want further details about Sayers Lake, call Bald Eagle State Park at 1-814-625-2775.

#18 SUSQUEHANNA RIVER (WEST BRANCH)

Keep in mind that the Susquehanna is one of the largest rivers in the east, and as with the Delaware, we will talk about its waters in several sections because it runs through a lot of area.

We will be brief here because the two primary fish are not "glamorous" in nature, although we bottom fishermen will fight you to the death if you try to compare your sissy bass with our two real "game fish."

The portion of the river in Area 3 is its Western Branch. The West Branch wanders through most of Clinton County with a

Bruce Stanton caught this 3 lb. smallmouth on the West Branch
of the Susquehanna River.

no-speed limit boat launch found at Lock Haven, and below this point, Bruce said the finest kind of carp action can be found.

Perhaps the easiest road to use when looking for the West Branch is 120 which follows most of the river until you get to Lockport, above Lock Haven.

While I couldn't find any evidence of stockings of channel catfish in 1999 or 2000, the western portion of the river holds lots of naturally reproducing channel's of very impressive size.

Near the town of Avis, at the southern end of Centre County, channel catfish seem to "Try Harder" (Sorry, I just couldn't avoid the pun). Seriously, channel catfish numbers and size were very impressive from Avis downstream since 1998.

Channel catfish will eat darn near anything, but if you have just come back from a trip down the shore in April, with a load of fresh mackerel, a chunk of fresh, smelly mackerel cannot possibly be beaten. Don't use fancy fillet strips for cat's. Instead, go with hunks of meat, with the section that runs across their lateral line the best. The middle part of the mackerel contains very dark meat and a piece cut from here will nearly always be gobbled by Mr. Whiskers.

So, fresh or frozen, stinky or just killed, mackerel for catfish, a formula for success!

If you happen across some non-game fish in the West Branch, like smallies and muskie-with walleye too, that's okay, just show respect to the carp and catfish.

Since I only gave you four "Best" spots in Area 3, let's tell you a little about some "Honorable Mention" waters now.

Trout lovers will find some fine fishing for brown trout in Penns Creek at the Catch and Release section, which is adjacent to Fish and Boat's field station #22 near the mouth of Cherry Run in Union County. Further, nearby at Ingleby, an All Tackle Trophy part can be found.

The Creek widens to the east below Glen Iron and a crossing can be found at Route 235.

Besides trout, the Atlas tells us that Penns Creek contains both bucket and bronzeback bass, as well as pike and muskie.

Another water worth discussing is Walker Lake in Snyder County, near Troxelville. Walker has some really big northern pike and walleye. Northerns were stocked here by Fish and Boat. Primary other residents are bullheads, sunnies and golden shiners (roach), but more than all others combined, a March, 2000 sampling found loads of black crappie.

For another good smaller lake, you may want to visit Black Moshannon in Centre County, 8 miles east of Phillipsburg. Found within Black Moshannon State Park, the lake is 250 acres in size.

Warmwater fish are featured here like largemouth bass, pike and pickerel, and a wide variety of panfish. The park offers facilities for fishing, boating, swimming, etc., try it!

CHAPTER 4

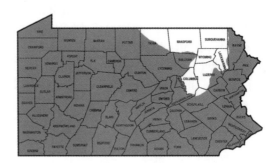

Area Four

L et's continue across the top of the state towards its far eastern side, stopping short of Wayne County. #4 includes some of Tioga, a small chunk of Schuykill, nearly all of Bradford, a little of Sullivan, most of Columbia, Luzerne and Lackawanna, and all of Susquehanna and Wyoming Counties.

Area Fisheries Technician Robert T. Wnuk wrote to me with some useful material about his "Best" two spots. In addition, Area 4 Manager Robert Moase talked about some good locations in the copy of 'Pennsylvania Angler and Boater' its editor Art Michaels sent to me.

Further, as you will see, I got still more data from other sources.

Let's start Area 4 with a location that is not under the jurisdiction of the state at all. In the two books I wrote with Ron Bern, "Gone Fishin' the 100 Best Spots in New Jersey," and "Gone Fishin' the 100 Best Spots in New York," we decided to at least share details about a few unique locations. If you read the start of this book carefully, you will remember me saying that I only wanted to talk about locations that are truly "Open to the Public." Ron and I skipped some great spots that were private, and I did the same thing here, with one exception.

We told you about three "Pay-Ponds" in the Garden State as well as about a Pay River out on Long Island. Now I will tell you about a Pay Lake in Pennsylvania, for a few reasons.

#19 BLYTHEBURN LAKE

In my outreach to better than 100 stores, one wrote back providing a great deal of help about Blytheburn Lake, and the name of that store was 'Gone Fishin' Baits and Supplies'. So, for several reasons, the site seemed like a winner. Not the least of which being the name of the source!

Seriously, when we talk about the "50 Best," I want you to be able to get a broad mix of fun, for experienced anglers and novices, as well as for the little people. A fast moving stream or monster loaded deep lake is not where little eight year old Jennifer should first be taken to. Instead, try a "Pay-Lake" like Blytheburn, she will love it!

Blytheburn Lake is in lower Luzerne County, at the little town of Mountain Top. You can find it a few miles off of Route 81 at exit 43. The store (Gone Fishin') is very close by.

Fifty acres of lake can be found here and its waters contain lots of fine game fish, with many a panfish to please the kids. Both large and smallmouth bass are in the lake, along with pickerel. It has crappie, bluegills, channel and bullhead catfish, plus carp. And, oh yes, tons of trout are stocked into the lake for your catching pleasure.

Daily, semi-annual or year-round fishing passes can be purchased. Rowboats, with or without electric motors, can be rented, or you can fish right from the shore. You may also launch your own rig for a fee. Normal safety regulations are in place and must be adhered to. Because it is a private lake, you do not have to have a Pennsylvania Fishing License, but of course, I hope you do, so that you can enjoy the wonderful fishing that Fish and Boat makes available to you clear across the state.

Kamloop trout were stocked in the lake, along with brookies in 1999 and 2000. Over in Jersey, the Round Valley Trout Association stocked a bunch of Kamloops in 2000 because they are both hard fighting fish as well as quick growing. They were only 12-13 inch-

Not just stocked trout, this pay lake offers bass too,
like this 7½ pounder.

es long that spring, but the one I caught on July 7th that year had
already reached 15 inches in length.

Trout generally want bait instead of lures here. Try chartreuse
Power Bait which is favored, as well as worms.

The store has a 24 hour bait machine available in case you have
a seasonal pass, and they are not open when you arrive.

Available too in the store were worms that became quite popular in 2000. One never knows when they will lose favor, but my
guess is that they will work well always. We are talking about a
normal night crawler that has been reared to contain a green color.
They actually glow in the dark, and are called Nitro-worms. Many
of my sources have told me that they work for bass!

#20 FRANCES SLOCUM LAKE

Known for its wonderful panfish population, watch out as you are reeling in a perch here, it could get very, very heavy as a muskie grabs hold! Fathead minnows are the top bait for perch and crappie, but remember, if the little fathead is eaten, the "eater" could shortly become the "eaten" too.

750 assorted fingerling sized muskies were added in 1999 to join with the rest of the population.

The lake is within Francis Slocum State Park, just off Route 309, between Kingston and Carverton, Luzerne County.

Besides perch and 'lunge, it holds small and largemouths, walleye, pickerel, rockbass, bluegills, and crappie. The primary forage consists of crayfish, alewives, leeches and freshwater shrimp.

Shore fishing can be found at one of the two boat ramps in the park, and at the other (daytime only), you may fish from shore or from the pier. The lake is electric motor only — or arm power. Leave the gas kickers at home.

Fishing Guide and Bait and Tackle man Ray Cichocki shared some of his wide knowledge of Frances Slocum with me.

Ray pointed out that in-season stocking of trout takes place here so that you can fish pre-season for other fish and not worry about being ticketed.

In the winter of 1989-90, Ray said he set a then ice fishing world record for muskies at Frances Slocum with his beast being nearly 50 inches long and 29½ pounds in weight. Five years later he caught a far bigger muskellunge at 39½ pounds!

The lake gets very narrow on the Carverton Road side and here is where Ray catches lots of panfish on little Charlie Brewer slider grubs with small twisters, as well as Bite Back Jigs. He does well too in front of the park in 12-15 foot brush piles.

Walleye enthusiasts do best after dark, and a trolled ½ ounce Krokodile-silver spoon produces, as well as ¼ ounce ball jigs that are tipped with night crawlers. For best 'eye results, troll along any rip-rap.

For bass, Ray prefers throwing Chompen hula grubs in watermelon seed color or black / blue rigged worms on a Bite Back Arkie head. He favors the handicapped access area where a 10-17 foot weed line can be found once the water warms up.

In addition to its launch sites, the park offers campsites and boat rentals. The handicapped dock is a wonderful feature.

#21 HAMMOND LAKE

And now let's head back west over to the 640 acre Hammond Lake in Tioga County. You may want to also try Tioga Reservoir directly to its east, but for now, let's stick to Hammond.

The reservoir is just south of the town of Tioga, off Route 287. Access to the lower lake can be obtained from Pennsylvania Fishing and Boating Map area 524, Ives Run. This site offers a launch ramp, dock, shore fishing as well as a pier. Ditto access area 525 to the north, called Campers Launch. It has all the services that Ives Run provides. Close by too is access area 566, aptly named Hammond Lake Access, another shore fishing spot.

The Atlas tells us that both Hammond and Tioga hold large-mouth bass, muskellunge (no longer stocked), walleye and black crappie, and doesn't differentiate between the two lakes. Bob Moase, however said that Tioga isn't as good as Hammond and has an acid mine drainage problem.

As for the crappie, Mr. Moase says that the lake doesn't have huge numbers, but those that are taken are generally very big, with 2 pound slabs not surprising anyone. Fishing pressure for them is modest as well. He wrote to say that a new black crappie record was set here with a 4.288 monster in 2000.

If you want the biggest kind of crappie, find an area inshore, which is both shallow and near wood. Use a small bobber with live bait, preferably something real lively.

While all the fish talked about above are nice to catch, the state again stocked Hammond with white / striped bass hybrids in 1999 and once they reach fighting weight an angler who hooks his first "Rocket" may just want to never catch anything else.

A survey taken by the state that year showed that the hybrids first stocked in 1995 had reached considerable size, with the largest they netted that year being 7.2 pounds. You will find that I really worship these hybrids in my book, but that is because, pound for pound, I have NEVER caught a fish that fights better. Just hook a 5 pounder at Hammond and you will know what I mean. Of course, the beast will probably break your line, but you can always blame it on a weak spot.

Gizzard shad were introduced into the lake some years back, and they make up the majority of the forage. To "Match the Hatch," try a "Thin-Fin" plug in purple and silver.

Also found in Hammond Reservoir are channel catfish with "double-figure" (10 pound or heavier) fish present. Smallies are also in the lake. Added summer features are some bald eagles and osprey.

#22 HARVEYS LAKE

The biggest natural lake by volume, covering 658 surface acres, this fine site can be reached off route 415, northwest of the borough of Dallas, due north of that same town, in Luzerne County.

Just as an example of what swims here, Fish and Boat stocked 4,000 trout in the lake before the opening gun of the 2000 season, and more than likely, an equal number mid-year too. Walleye were also stocked.

The Atlas tells us that Harveys also contains large and small-mouth bass, plus perch and pickerel.

There are at least three access sites to the lake. A boat ramp may be used at Grotto Marina, which also has a dock. The D.O.T. maintains a site at the very southern tip of Route 415 and a ramp can be found here. Fish and Boat has a facility as well, between the two just discussed. It allows shore fishing and also has a ramp and dock.

Perhaps the single thing you need to learn about Harveys Lake is that a lot of other people already know about it! That does not mean that you should avoid it, simply that you need to pick and choose the day you hit the lake. As with many other large bodies of water, a wise angler might want to stay away on, say July 4th, okay? Ditto just about every weekend day in the summer.

I received a letter from Robert T. Wnuk, Area 4 Fisheries

18 inch smallie caught and released by guide Ray Cichocki
at Harveys Lake.

Technician, and he provided wonderful material about the lake.

While it has the three access points talked about, most of the lake shoreline is private, and has lots of cottages around it so you do need to know that it is not very shoreline friendly. Other than a few spots, Harveys is a boat lake!

Spring and fall are the best times of the year to fish here. If you hit it in the summer, try to fish it early. The fishing is generally better then, and most "Sunday Sailor's" will still be sleeping off the night before anyway. An alternate would be evening fishing.

The two main targets on the lake are smallmouth bass (Guide Ray Cichocki often brings customers here for smallies), and brown trout.

The lake contains lots of wood and weed, with some rocks, and old wood cribs along with old ash piles from when the old steam ferry's used to travel the lake.

Ray swears by the use of a good pair of Hobie polarized sunglasses to see the weedlines he is after. And since I fished with him and he saw stuff I never spotted, it wasn't just his better eyesight, it had to be his glasses.

Favoring the shady side of shallow docks for largemouth at Harveys, Ray catches more smallies at docks that are in deeper, rocky water.

Mr. Wnuk told me that one of the Waterways Conservation Officers checked a 13 pound brown trout that was caught in the lake on 5/23/00! This is a Special Regulation lake for trout and as of 2000, it called for a daily limit of three fish with only one in the excess of 18 inches.

Because they feed so well, brown trout fatten up like footballs at Harveys Lake and we hear that fish which hold over one year, average 5 pounds!

Most anglers fish for browns with flat lines and planer boards during the spring, and with downriggers during the summer. Read your fish finder to locate them when the water really warms up and set your ball to swim your lure just above that mark.

Most trout will swim up to a plug or spoon rather than down, thus the need to have your "bait" be a little high up.

Now when it comes to smallmouth bass, the lake really is excellent with large numbers of chunky bronzebacks in the 15-18 inch class. These fish are generally caught by anglers fishing shoreline structure, with jigs and top water baits.

Motor horsepower is not limited at Harveys so, again, try to fish it in more quiet times.

#23 SUSQUEHANNA RIVER (NORTH BRANCH)

Back in Area 3, we talked about the West Branch of the Susquehanna. Realize please that at least one entire book has already been written about the Susquehanna, so if you are truly interested in reading in greater detail about the entire vast length of the river, I suggest you buy the book.

In this Area, we will talk about the rivers' North Branch, which enters Pennsylvania from New York at Great Bend in Susquehanna County at the northeastern most part of Area 4. Fisheries Technician Robert Wnuk said that the river travels for approximately 5 miles from its entry point, then returning to New York. It finally makes up its' mind to return to the Keystone State near Milltown from where it flows approximately 178 more miles to its confluence with its' West Branch where Area 4 ends, and Area 3 begins.

In addition to its' walleye and smallmouth population, muskellunge too are found in the North Branch. From the data that State Stocking Coordinator Marguerite Davidson sent to me, I counted not less than 8,750 fingerling muskies stocked in just the North Branch in 1999!

1998 samplings of the North Branch showed good numbers of walleye. Area Manager Robert Moase said that the 1995 walleye year-class fish probably reached as much as 20 inches by 1999 and by now, far longer.

In fact, Moase was quoted as saying that 1998 was "phenomenal" because the winter was mild and anglers caught them all winter long. He said that 30 inch and larger fish were caught that season. Even more impressive was the report from a Conservation Officer that a 38 inch 'eye was taken!

You can get a free copy of the State's Fishing and Boating Map, (which was a great help to me overall). On it you will be able to find some of the many access areas that are managed by Fish and Boat. In addition, numerous private and municipal spots can be found.

Three well known Fish and Boat ramps can be reached in Bradford County. They are called Sayre, Wysox and Terrytown. Each allows unlimited horsepower motors and shore fishing is allowed nearby.

As Technician Wnuk said, "Smallmouth bass are the bread and

butter on the North Branch."

Few trophy sized smallies are caught, but the bass are quite numerous and 50 fish evenings during the summer are common. Most of the bass range from 9 inches to 14.

Mr. Wnuk also told us that muskellunge are found throughout the entire river but hot spots are generally located at the mouths of major tributaries. He echoed Manager Moase's sentiments too regarding walleye, saying that they are caught all year round but are best from November through February.

If you can take the cold, fish for walleye at night. Just remember to fish with a buddy because a winter flop could result in an injury you could not walk away from. If someone is with you, help could be obtained.

Other fish in the North Branch? Well, channel catfish are commonly caught along with carp and suckers.

For the Honorable Mention in Area 4, let me suggest Lily Lake in Luzerne County, home to lots of trophy sized chain pickerel as well as big northern pike, and plenty of panfish.

CHAPTER 5

Area Five

T his Area picks up the entire northeastern part of the State, running down the Delaware River from Wayne, clear through all of Northampton Counties. It encompasses the Lehigh River drainage down to the Delaware River, and up the river to where it reaches the New York border. All or part of ten counties are covered and the main man for the State here is David A. Arnold, who not only wrote to me but also helped define a few things over the phone. Let me remind you again that we are following the alphabet in the interest of simplicity, okay?

#24 BLACK CREEK

State Game Lands #40 would be your goal to find this excellent Carbon County Wild Trout wonderland. Routes 476 and 80 both go through it, and 940 is just above the Creek at the town of Leonardville. For more help in locating Black Creek, it's above Hickory Run State Park (which also has fine trout water called Hickory Run).

Mr. Arnold reported in 'Angler and Boater's ' first edition of the 1999 year that it's a fairly solid, strong stream from year to year — with a lot of nice size distribution, with most occupants being stream-bred brownies.

Three commission biologist samplings on Black Creek were taken the summer of 1999 and according to the report given, sections sampled near SR0534 and above it's confluence with Fourth Run, showed 527 trout in total. A little 110 yard stretch alone yielded 105 brownies and one was a wild fish that pulled the tape out to 23.8 inches long!

Of course, most were the typical 7-12 inch fish, but still this creek is worth listing in our "50 Best." I hope that you will agree after you fish it a few times.

#25 DELAWARE RIVER (WEST BRANCH)

Arguably, if you omit the tributaries of Lake Erie and their superb population of steelhead trout, what many call "THE BEST" trout waters in Pennsylvania can be found on the West Branch of the Delaware River.

The Eastern branch flows through New York and joins with Pennsylvania's West Branch at the New York town of Hancock, and from there on down, we have the river itself, to be discussed in great length shortly.

For now, let's try to picture ourselves fishing any or all of the eight miles this piece of water covers. It's way up at the northeastern tip of the State. Game Lands #299 in Wayne County is a fine access point. The best road to reach it is SR4014 and the town nearby is Balls Eddy.

Dave Arnold told me that much of the Branch is wadeable, with its widest part when full reaching 288 feet across.

Known for its superb population of wild trout, with brown and rainbow the feature performers, Delaware River Park Ranger Dave Bank said that it also contains some really big walleyes as well as smallmouth bass. In fact, Mr. Arnold added that the West Branch features shad in the spring that leave the main body and head west up into this stretch.

Fish and Boat maintains an access site north of the stream at the Shehawken Creek mouth, and small boats like canoes and rafts are seen wandering downstream. Besides this easy entry you can also walk through Game Lands #299 to reach parts of the Branch that few bother fishing.

We warn you though, that this section contains bears, so if you are not very fleet afoot, you might be better off entering through the more conventional public access points.

The bottom line is that if you want a shot at trophy sized trout, in wonderful, scenic surroundings, fish the West Branch of the Delaware River. You'll like it!

Arnold said this water is Artificial Only, so leave the worms at home, but don't forget to bring your camera if you are more into Catch and Release than keepers. The color of these wild fish in the fall is truly remarkable, especially those putting on their spawning flash.

#26 DELAWARE RIVER — AREA FIVE SECTION

This stretch of the river runs from the northeast tip of Pennsylvania in Wayne County, across from Hancock, NY, all the way down through the Delaware Water Gap and then to Bucks County where we will pick it up again in Area 6.

Pennsylvania residents and visitors alike would find a trip to one of my main sources of information about the river quite useful. Anglers Roost can be found in Lackawaxen and here one or more of the Clan Zaimes can usually be found. The Zaimes' offer raft, canoe, tube and kayak rentals at the store, as well as a wide variety of tackle. Advice is free!

Charlie Zaimes was the Editor of the old 'Anglers News' and he and his son Dimitri had operated too out of Margate, NJ, before deciding to spend most of their time in Lackawaxen.

Charlie sat down and wrote to me about the river. He said that the Upper Delaware in Pike County and its tributaries from Calicoon, NY, down to the Delaware Water Gap offer a true smorgasbord of fishing. Smallmouth bass, walleye, trout, shad, muskellunge, carp, bluegills, sucker and catfish all provide a menu that will have just about every angler salivating.

The annual spawning run of shad draws hundreds of anglers to the Upper Delaware from late April to mid or late June. Most of them use spinning tackle from shore but a few still throw flies.

Shad darts or flutter spoons are favored on spinning gear, from shore or boat, but a big move started in the late '90's to fool shad on the light wand with streamers.

I fished the river right below the Route 80 Bridge with Dave Bank and his style was typical of the real shad pros. We anchored in fast water and he put two rods in off of downriggers. The balls held flutter spoons down right near the bottom and if you watched carefully enough, you could see the very first tap and pull the line out of the snap and stick the silver beauties. Soft of mouth, the snap actually helps control your desire to remove the head of the fish on your set. Thus struck, a shad usually gets away but with a downrigger controlling your power, a better chance at bringing the fish in is achieved.

Joe Kasper, perhaps the most experienced Delaware River angler I know, tells me that he favors using in-line sinkers to down-riggers, because he feels that this method offers a more natural approach to catching mid-level shad.

Zaimes said that boat and shore fishing are equally productive, and the Pennsylvania side of the river is fairly shallow with wading available in most places.

There are a number of boat launching areas on both the New York and Pennsylvania shores. New York has free launch ramps in Narrowsburg and at the Ten Mile River Access Area, six miles south of Narrowsburg on State Road 97.

Free launch sites in the Keystone State are found way up at Balls Eddy on down to Milford. Perhaps the most popular ramp is near Anglers Roost, on Scenic Drive, directly in front of the Zane Grey Museum, once the home of the noted author and outdoor writer.

You can find the museum, as well as the ramp and Anglers Roost, 25 miles upstream from Port Jervis, NY. Take NY Route 97 North to Minisink Ford. Turn left over the Roebling Bridge into Pennsylvania to get there.

The Zane Grey Pool is at the confluence of the Delaware and the Lackawaxen Rivers. You may want to take a side trip up to the Lackawaxen itself too. More on that in the Honorable Mention part of this area.

Heavy (¼ ounce) darts are the lure of choice for most shad anglers downstream from The Gap, where the fish hunker near the bottom. Knowledgeable fishermen have discovered that the shad will strike lures at or near the surface in the Upper River, and they've switched to much smaller darts and spoons, as small as $\frac{1}{32}$ ounce.

The Portland Power Plant is the first place to look for up river shad due to its discharge of warm water, so make sure to check this place out on weekdays. (Too crowded otherwise).

In the early days of shad fishing (the 50's), most bait shops sold darts painted with a red head and white body. Since then, Charlie wrote, we've seen major changes in color; chartreuse, fluorescent orange, green, purple, blue, black, yellow, pearl and gold to name a few. When Zaimes is asked which color he prefers, his standard reply is "Use whatever color you like, as long as it's red and white!"

The very best time for walleye fishing is when they spawn, January through March. (I near froze to death one day with Dave Bank, trying for them up around Poxano, but all we caught were two little yellow perch that day).

Although many portions of the river are frozen in the winter, the Zane Grey Pool where the Lackawaxen River joins "The Big D," remains open most of the time. In February, of 1999, Dimitri Zaimes weighed Ron Miele's 14¼ pound 'eye!

Smallmouth bass and largemouths were legal in the Upper River the year 'round (make sure this hasn't changed by reading the Summary!). The ideal times are from June through November. Although there are some trophy sized largemouth bass in the river, the bronzebacks outnumber their cousins by unbelievable proportions.

They can be caught on a wide variety of baits like shiners, helgrammites, worms, mealies, grasshoppers and beetles, but Dave Bank swears by self-netted fallfish, often mistakenly called "chub."

He drifts downstream, letting his bait bounce along the bottom in the current, until a bass stops by. The born in the river fallfish make the best bait going. When you get down river in Area 6, the bait of choice changes to killies, but up north, try fallfish if you can net them yourself. Other choices are crawfish and leeches.

As for lures, Zaimes suggests the old standby CP Swing, or Rooster Tail. Other spinners he fishes are Thomas Rough Rider, Blue Fox Vibrax, Phoebe, Mepps (with Squirrel Tail), and a Johnson Silver Minnow tipped with an Uncle Josh Ripple-Rind strip.

Fly fishermen are really taking to smallmouth bass. Trout jump, to be sure, but smallies often jump higher, especially those that have gotten so strong by fighting the often fierce currents of the Delaware.

Streamers of choice are orange and brown Clouser Minnows. In the summer, for dries, try Light Cahill, Sulphur, Blue Wing Olive or Adams in sizes 12 or 14.

There are a number of Class 1 and Class 2 rapids in the Upper River and all are home to some mighty hefty trout, mostly rainbow and brown. One of the most productive is Cedar Rapids, two miles downstream of Lackawaxen. There's a half-mile run below the rapids, a deep channel on the New York side of the river. 20+ inch rainbow trout are commonly caught in this pool on deep running spoons.

According to Dave Arnold, anglers who are targeting Delaware River's muskellunge population, would be well served if they try the Lackawaxen, Smithfield and I-80 pools.

Needless to say, bigger is usually better. If you can get a half-pound sucker, do try it. However, Dave Bank has had several muskies inhale his little three inch fallfish too.

The portion of the "Big D" that is in Area 5, runs all the way down to Easton and every fish (other than trout) discussed so far are caught throughout, including some of the biggest submarine sized carp you ever saw!

Please do understand that we cannot very well cover the whole river alone in Area 5 and 6. Several books are in print that are devoted solely to the Delaware and we suggest you find one in your local library and check it out.

#27 DUCK HARBOR POND

Well, we now go from one of the biggest bodies of water in the State to a far smaller and less known spot, but one that is a fine location to try.

Duck Harbor Pod was a 74 acre natural lake in Wayne County which was increased to 122 acres in size some years back by the construction of a small dam.

To reach the lake you can take either 1) SR0371 in Lebanon Township to Township Road T617, or 2) SR0191 in Damascus Township to T676.

Dave Arnold tells us that the lake offers a well-rounded fishery for yellow perch, walleye, smallmouth bass, trout, bluegills and brown bullhead. The Atlas adds that largemouth bass and pickerel also live here.

A 14 inch minimum size limit was in place as of 2000 for brown trout, which are stocked each spring in both catchable and fingerling size.

If you are using bait for trout, please make sure to carry a sharp pair of scissors with you. If your hook is not visible, and you either don't want to take one home or it is under the size limit, cut your line! I have caught many a trout that had more than one hook inside, and if properly cut off, they live quite well. My hook of choice with live herring is a size 6, 3906 Mustad and I guess I have cut off over 1,000 hooks that were swallowed.

For those of you who think that this is not possible, try to remember friends and family members who have artificial joints, tooth implants, etc., and you will realize that a fish can survive with ease, just like a human can.

The main forage at Duck Harbor Pond is alewife herring.

Walleye are stocked in the lake. Just as an example, 6,000 were added in 1999 and these were not "fry," but rather an assortment of somewhat larger "fingerling" size.

A boat ramp can be found in the southern tip of the lake.

#28 LITTLE LEHIGH RIVER

Situated in Lehigh County, is Little Lehigh Creek / River. Don't

*No sirree, not for me — but as you can see,
the Little Lehigh is always open!*

confuse it with the Lehigh Canal or the Lehigh River though, these
are different bodies of water. Both receive trout stockings, and the
river itself is stocked with substantial numbers of muskellunge,
walleye and even shad.

Here again is Trout Country, WILD TROUT COUNTRY. As a
reporter for the 'Fishermen Magazine', I was often told about the
superb action available the entire year on the Little Lehigh, but it
wasn't until I decided to write this book that I got more deeply into
the subject. To obtain the most substantial volume of data for you, I
called Dan Buss at 'The Sports Shops at Nestor's', in Whitehall, Pa.

He and others often told me about the volume of trout that could
be caught here, as well as how great the access is. Now I know that
many of you don't mind back-packing the Colorado River or other
far off spots, but while the Little Lehigh allows you to walk in, you

can also pull your car up alongside and throw your flies until your arm falls off.

Much of the Little Lehigh can be found in Allentown, west of the main body of the Lehigh River. Dan Buss said that to reach it from the Northeast Extension of the Pennsylvania Turnpike, you take Route 22 East to Route 309 South to Route 29 South (Cedar Crest Blvd.). Then go approximately 2/10 of a mile and make a left turn onto Fish Hatchery Road. When you get to the bottom of the hill you will cross the Little Lehigh!

This is the upstream part of the Heritage Trout Angling Section, which extends on down one mile. Regulations here require fly fishing only with barbless hooks. It's No-Kill!

You are not allowed to wade from Fish Hatchery Road to Firemen's Bridge. From Firemen's Bridge down, you may, to the lower reaches near the Oxford Drive Bridge.

The Little Lehigh is a 30-50 foot wide limestone spring fed creek which does not freeze in the winter and stays nice and cold all summer long due to its' constant feed.

Nearly five miles of the creek flows through the Allentown Park System which is well maintained and easy to find. A jogging /bike path parallels both sides of the stream. The Heritage Section draws the largest number of fly fishermen. Upstream and down, the open water offers less crowded conditions and fish that are less selective.

The stream receives ample stocking by the State and a Fish and Game association too. There are many angling opportunities available to fishermen with bait or spinning lures, but it is the fly fishing that the stream is most famous for.

The majority of the fish here are stream bred wild brownies. It's placid pools and numerous insect hatches make it a dry fly fishers dream.

The warmer days of January and February are when you can find trout feeding on midges. Effective patterns include Al's Rats, Griffith Gnats and Emerging Midges in size 24-32. We get to slightly bigger flies in March and early April when afternoon hatches of Blue Wing Olives occur — go with sizes 18 or 20.

As we reach the middle of April, Crain flies start to appear. Try yellow or tan in #18 or size 16 orange Crains. As the month ends, sporadic 18 and 20 tan Caddis hatches occur during the day.

May is Sulphur Season, with late afternoon hatches of Pale Evening Duns in huge numbers. To match the hatch, go with emergers, traditional, parachutes or size 16 brown spinners.

For the next month the fly of choice is a size 18 Sulphur emerger, traditional or parachute. Once we get into summer, Dan suggests terrestrials like 14-18 ants or beetles, and Jassids in 18-22.

A Trico hatch also starts around July 4th and from then on until September you can count on hatches of them occurring every morning from 8-10am. The Little Lehigh is a premier Trico stream and fishermen come from far away to fish it. The hatch is tremendous and good patterns include male and female Trico Duns or spinners in 22-26. As noted in the above paragraph, ants and beetles work great too, so if a Trico doesn't do it, go terrestrial.

From the end of the summer through October, a showering of 20-24 Blue Wing Olives appear.

The advice for the rest of the calendar year for you may not be taken well, but since Dan gave you so much help, please take his suggestion now to keep off until nearly January. These two months are spawning time, so let's rest them to allow for reproduction and wonderful fishing to follow.

#29 PROMISED LAND LAKE

And now for a spot that is available to just about everybody, one that offers darn near everything! Park Ranger Dave Bank says that Promised Land is "One of the jewels in the crown of the State Parks System!"

Promised Land State Park can be found in Pike County, 10 miles north of Candadensis, along Route 390.

Within the park are two lakes and several streams. The bigger lake, Promised Land Lake, is 422 acres in size and to its west you will find the 173 acre Lower Lake.

The park itself is a true 365 day a year place to visit. Whether it's summer or winter sports that you seek, all can be found in this location.

7½ pound chain pickerel caught at Promised Land Lake
by Greg Price.

In the winter, the ice fishing can be simply incredible. While the lakes hold both small and largemouth bass, along with muskellunge, pickerel and catfish, the hot shots like Park Ranger Dave Bank fish here for yellow perch and big, fat sunnies. And the time they do this is right in the dead of the winter, through hard water! Mr. Arnold did point out that special panfish regulations exist here, so check your Summary for size and bag limits.

Dave has often told me of the superb action he finds through the ice with a small jig, tipped with bait. When available, his bait of choice is a live grub, common to the area. Worms — garden, baby nightie and mealie, all work also. A mousee is another good addition. He sometimes sets a few tip-ups with shiners for pickerel while jigging a hole for the tasty panfish. They sure stay fresh after being caught because they generally freeze solid. (Did you ever see a "perchsicle"?) Dave has, plenty of them.

Bank has caught some wonderful bass and pickerel in the lakes at more sane times. But the way he drools when he talks about ice fishing on Promised Land's lakes makes me try to remember that it may not be an altogether bad idea to go out and freeze your tail off catching ½ pound fish.

The park contains approximately 3,000 acres overall, and is surrounded by 12,350 acres of spectacular state forest.

The bigger lake has a swimming beach and boat rental. Three boat ramps are there and two more are in Lower Lake.
Not commonly found, one of the big lake ramps has a fishing pier as well. The lakes are electric only.

So what do you want to do? Picnic, certainly — 200 tables are in place. Hunt? 450 acres are open to hunters in season. Next to Lower Lake are a dozen rustic rental cabins.

Hikers, foot powered bikers and folks bringing in their own horses can all have a ball in the park too. And in the winter, snowmobilers also are allowed in designated areas.

If your mate is fishing through ice and that is not your thing, cross-country skiing can be done.

So the message is "Get Thee to The Promised Land!"

#30 LAKE WALLENPAUPACK

Wallenpaupack may be the most heavily fished lake in the state, but if you pick and choose carefully, you should be able to enjoy yourself and not be made crazy by the speed boaters that frequent the big lake all summer long.

This may be the lake that gets more fish stocked in it than any other. Just to illustrate, this 5,700 acre Pike and Wayne County impoundment received stockings of 14,000 channel catfish, 199,500 walleye, 103,400 true strain stripers and 51,000 hybrid bass in a recent year. These were fingerlings too, not "small fry."

A pickerel was caught through the ice in the Ledgedale area by Mike Hrabina, which weighed nearly 7 pounds. He was using a medium shiner on a tip up. An example of the big channel cat's that swim in the lake is a photo of Tommy Seas, in 'Pa. Angler and Boater', Second issue of 2000. His cat weighed 10½ pounds.

I counted seven access sites to the lake in my free copy of the Commission's Fishing and Boating Map. Area Fisheries Manager Arnold told me about the free ramp that the state maintains on the

Four huge stripers caught in May at Wallenpaupack.

lake's northern shoreline near the dam. Fishing is permitted from shore here too, and although the lake is quite huge, remember this spot, because not much stand and fish access is available on the lake — it's mostly for boat people.

The lake was constructed by Pennsylvania Power and Light in 1926 to supply electricity during peak demand periods. While the lake is ringed with homes, having personally seen and fished it, it is NOT unsightly because local Zoning Boards did not allow homes built to stand on stilts in the water. Most houses are a bit uphill, and not eye clutter to us.

PP&L provides four public boat accesses for a nominal fee at Wilsonville, Caffery, Ironwood Point, and Ledgedale. Wilsonville and Ironwood each also offers camp sites. Again, shoreline fishing is permitted, but in somewhat small spaces.

The lake's big fish community consists of brown trout, walleye, both true strain and hybrid striped bass, chain pickerel, large and smallmouth bass, carp and channel catfish. Smaller but plentiful are yellow perch, brown and yellow bullheads, suckers, and not less than six varieties of sunfish, with rock bass being most common.

The best action for numbers of good sized fish come from both varieties of stripers, smallies, brown trout, and channel cat's. Top panfish catches are made with yellow perch, rock bass and bluegills.

As with many big lakes, the dominant forage fish is again alewives, thus any artificial lure that resembles an alewife should do fine.

Due to low level mercury problems, the state has advised anglers to not eat walleyes that are 19 inches long or better. I found that this problem discussed too way up in Vermont on the Connecticut River on all sizes of walleye!

In the summer, mid-evening to mid-morning are the best times when the lake is crowded. But before Memorial Day, or after Labor Day, you should do fine any weekday, all the rest of the year.

Striper lovers pound the lake all May long during the day and the fellows who know the lake catch quite a few big bass then. In the summer, it's night or never though.

Dave Arnold said that the Fish and Boat launch area is good for walleye, stripers and brownies. Stripers can also be caught at Ironwood Point and just west of Ledgedale in the next bay/cove area. If you are looking for walleye and channel catfish, they are everywhere, but Arnold feels that the best areas for channel's are in the eastern half of the main lake. He is confident that Wallenpaupack's channel cat's have already reached bigger than 20 pounds.

Smallmouth bass are probably the most sought after and caught game fish in the lake. 12-16 inchers are very common and fat fish that nearly make a foot and a half long weigh 3 pounds or more.

I fished one afternoon into evening on a mid-summer Monday with well known guide Ray Cichocki and it was quite apparent that he really loves his hobby. (Besides his obvious skill, he never ate anything, a true sign of a real fishing nut!)

Weeds were the hiding place and medium shiners drifted through were the style. Using a split shot or two, we caught a variety of fish and in all, my guess is that the total score was in excess of 30. Remember too, this was summer and the big boats were

Frank Deeches and John Berger caught these two walleye and big "Rocket" with guide Ray Cichocki on Lake Wallenpaupack.

buzzing nearby.

We put 17 or 18 smallies back, five pickerel, a perch, and maybe ten rock bass. The bass jumped like bass do, the chain's dug deep as they often do, and the two anglers enjoyed themselves, just like two serious anglers are also supposed to do!

If you want to hire a guide who really knows his lake, (and Ray also guides on Harveys Lake), call him at 1-570-654-9555 or 1-570-654-5436.

Ray breaks the lake down into four seasons. In the Spring he fishes the warmest water, the shallowest sections where the river enters. He keys in on water that receives the most sunlight like 5 Mile Creek, Ledgedale River, and Ironwood Point.

When the water warms, he starts working toward the front of the lake on to the White Beauty, Millbrook and Capri areas. Then over to the dike where he picked me up, and over to Walts Cove.

As autumn approaches Ray looks for schools of bait fish toward the lakes many coves. They will be in rocky water or hiding in the weeds.

Once it gets really cold the lake will have turned over and most big fish will be out in deep water, coming in periodically to feed too. His ice lure of choice would be a Krocodile jig.

You can pick up brochures about the lake if you visit his mom's tackle store in Dupont ("Ray's). Ray may very well be out guiding anglers on the lake, but someone will be watching the store, probably his mom.

Honorable Mention: This area contains wonderful trout streams as well as many a lake that is worthy of mentioning. Included in the list are:

Fairview Lake — in Pike County. It's just south of Lake Wallenpaupack, so remember that if "Paupack" is crowded. Alewife herring are the main food for the population of game fish found in the lake. They consist of big and smallmouth bass, pickerel and pike. Lots of yellow perch and sunnies are here as well, and Fish and Boat has a gas motor boat launch on the Southwest corner of the lake (reached via SR 0390, north from I-84 to SR 4004).

Lackawaxen River — in Wayne and Pike County, as briefly discussed by our friend Charles Zaimes in the Upper Delaware section, is another fine body of water. It received 18,400 trout before the Opening Day of 2000 alone! Charlie told me it gets 26,000 brown and 'bow yearly, and many trout naturally reproduce here as well. The 15 mile stretch of the "Lackie" from Lackawaxen to Hawley is very wadeable and even on Opening Day, is not crowded. Lures of all kinds work, ditto bait.

Saucon Creek — in Northampton County. A 2.1 mile stretch was changed to Artificial Lures Only in 1997. Sites sampled in the summer of 1999 included High Street in Hellertown and at Saucon Park in Bethlehem. Found in total were well over 1,000 trout. Most were wild brownies, but some were stocked rainbows which migrated down from Bingen.

Shohola Lake — in Pike County. This large (1,137 acres) man-made lake is on State Game Lands No. 180 in Shohola Township. Created in 1967 to help with waterfowl production, the lake is now a fine place to fish too. It has three electric motor only launch sites. Shallow, it holds a wide variety of panfish, as well as pickerel and largemouth bass. It's an excellent ice fishing lake, with pickerel the primary target.

And we haven't even touched on the Lehigh River itself, or Beltzville Lake in Carbon County. Boy, I don't know how Dave Arnold covers so much territory. Maybe in my next book?

CHAPTER 6

———◆◆———

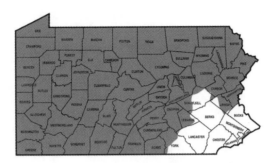

Area Six

A nd now we get to the south east part of Pennsylvania, reaching through Bucks County, and down the Delaware River, wrapping back around to the Counties of Lancaster and York, through which much of the Susquehanna flows. All or part of 11 counties are in Area 6, and this section is under the fine supervision of Michael L. Kaufmann who, like his peers, provided a great amount of assistance to me. He even proof-read my copy and offered corrections.

#31 DELAWARE RIVER (AREA SIX SECTION)

As we get below Easton, we break into Bucks County, and within the 50.4 miles that flow downstream to Morrisville, a wide variety of fish are available. Once we get below Morrisville, across from Trenton, different rules start to apply as the river becomes tidal. Mr. Kaufmann covers the 50+ miles noted above and that is a long beat indeed.

If you don't live in a cave, you already know about the famous Lambertville Shad Festival held yearly across the river. They worship shad on that side of the river, but in Easton, a quite successful shad derby occurs annually.

Shad are taken throughout this entire stretch with the Mercer

*Helen trying to keep cool with her 9/98 Area 6 smallie
in the Delaware.*

Power Plant on the other side of the river below Trenton being the
spot that they all start biting at. The artificially warmed water here
is the spot to fish, but do try to avoid the weekends. In spite of the
cold of April, it gets crowded.

Mr. Kaufmann was careful to point out that boaters need to exercise extreme caution when running down river because the water gets quite shallow at certain points. For example, when you get to stream outfalls and fast water appears, this could be an area where your motor bottoms out.

In particular, he said that the Wing Dam at Lumberville (Bulls Island State Park, Raven Rock, is on the other side), is tough to manage. I have seen boaters slam down river here, half-disappearing and then popping up again, but it is not for me. A small opening exists, but again, caution please! The dam in New Hope/Lambertville is very famous among striped bass and shad enthusiasts, but the downstream access on the Pa. side can present severe hazards, so again, be careful.

The predominant fish found here include smallmouth bass, channel, and white catfish, striped bass (mostly late Spring through Summer), redbreast sunfish, plus shad and herring (April, May and early June).

Shad anglers like to anchor their boats just downstream of bridge abutments, or below outcroppings of rocks at the exits of streams. The changing flow of water caused at these areas are often the top places to pick off some shad.

Remember that Joe Kasper gets many of them with in-line sinkers holding his flutter spoon or dart down part way, so don't just go with a downrigger style of angling.

If you want herring, either to eat or for bait, the Delaware probably has more herring running upstream to spawn than any other waterway in the East. Fish for them where water depths change, and of course, the style is a gold hook or two or three, etc., held down with a dipsey sinker of appropriate weight. If you cast across the current and sweep back during your retrieve, and don't catch herring, you are probably not using a heavy enough weight. The sinker must bounce bottom for best results.

Sabiki rigs, pre-tied deals that look like a bunch of small white flies, have taken over where simple gold hooks left off, and they sure do produce good numbers of herring.

Striped bass sharpies will catch a herring on one rod and quickly hook it on a heavier stick, casting out for striped bass. A live her-ring is often the best bait you can use for the bigger stripers, some-times even better than a live eel.

If you like saltwater fishing down the Jersey shore, fillet some herring and save them for strip baits.

I have personally seen a muskellunge, caught one pickerel, and even a lone trout in this stretch, and if you want suckers, try the Lumberville area in the winter, from a double anchored boat while using a baby night crawler on bottom. Fun to catch, they bend the rod and when it is cold out, it beats the boob-tube. My personal best in this area was a fully 4 pounder caught late in March of 2000.

Of course, in the winter, carp have no respect for other fish, and this is the time of the year that they really turn carnivorous, with worms making up the majority of their diet. My friend Ron Bern has taken two 20+ pounders in the winter on worm in this imme-diate vicinity.

Kaufmann points out that public boat ramps can be found in Pennsylvania at Easton, Upper Black Eddy, Tinicum Township, (Uhlerstown) and down in Yardley. Several exist too across the river.

The food of choice in this part of the river is pretty much the same as above, fallfish, but as you get further south, the streams contain thousands of killies and the fish love these very hardy bait-fish. In addition, after they spawn, small shad and herring come down river and they are inhaled in great numbers, especially by bass, those with stripes and those without.

Mike told me that crawfish are found in the river and the fish also like to eat American eels. Special netting regulations are in place for collection of eels though, so if you want to try some for bait, I strongly suggest you buy them from an approved tackle store.

Talking about eels, what some feel is the number one place to catch big stripers from shore on the river, is at the Wing Dam at New Hope/Lambertville, and here is when an angler using live eels can really produce.

You don't have to be jealous of the boaters if you head hook a live eel and release it downstream, live-lined, at the dam. Just make sure you have sturdy tackle though, because some of the stripers caught range up to 20+ pounds! This fishing is not written about much, but it goes on during the late Spring and right into most of the Summer.

The further south you get into the river, the more scary the health advisories exist. Once again, I don't want you to take these warnings lightly, but since the book is about fishing and not eating, hesitate on the side of caution. Read The Summary about the fish found in the lower river, but practicing Catch and Release could be helpful for your health, not only for the fish you put back.

#32 DELAWARE RIVER — TIDAL!!

Not covered by the freshwater guys, once you get below Morrisville, different rules and regulations apply and other folks have jurisdiction. Out of Mike Kaufmann's "beat" is this very long stretch, and it is certainly worth talking about (Remember though, whole books have been written about "The Big D" , so don't think I am covering it completely!).

The brackish water fishing in the Delaware includes both fresh and saltwater species. The "sweet" water fish are mostly large-mouth bass, crappies, and catfish — and plenty are available.

I stopped by at Brinkman's Bait and Tackle in Philadelphia in my quest for first hand details, and met with Bruce, who was quite helpful.

He suggests striper fishing this area behind the U.P.S. Plant, in South Philadelphia, from shore. This is bank fishing, with lots of free parking, and a six foot tide change occurs. Go with the last three hours in and first three hours of outgoing tide in this spot. As we point out below, though, remember that much of this area is Catch and Release for several months.

Try the Dredge Harbor to Riverton part of North Philadelphia, for bucketmouth's and stripers, with schools of calico often sitting just off bottom above the structure. Largemouth bass specialists fish around the old broken piers found nearby, with spinner baits or plastics.

*Joe DiPento lost half his head while netting these 31 and 18 inch
stripers that he caught on one lure (a Pencil Popper)
at the same time, in the tidal waters of the Delaware.*

Channel catfish and striped bass are the two really big fish found
and myriads of white perch swim throughout, even down into pure
salt.

While live eels or herring, as well as blood worms produce
super catches of striped bass, some of the hot shots will catch
white perch and use them for bait. That is really "Match the hatch"
and it definitely works!

Anglers fish for striped bass by tide. Some swear that the last
two hours of incoming and first hour of outgoing are best. What all
seem to agree on is that, if you are anchored near an island, you
want to be on the other side of it from the tide. For example, if the
tide is chugging out, anchor behind it and fish downstream for best
results.

The waters off the old Philadelphia Navy Yard are very popular. The "ringers" fish here at night and clean up. Some use blood-worms and others go with live eels. Guys chop the head of the eel off and use just it alone. They stand the "risk" though of catching monster sized channel catfish on an eel head, instead of a big striper.

Still another well liked site for stripers can be found near the Philadelphia Airport, using the same style.

Many an angler after both channel's and bass will anchor down-stream of the variety of bridges that cross from Trenton and below. Bait fishermen do very well, but here a carefully tossed jig will catch fish too.

In the late Spring, thousands of small striped bass go on the feed and light tackle enthusiasts will catch double-headers on a small plug or jig with a teaser tied above it. The bigger bass like Bomber Long A's.

Please note that the 2000 Summary of Rules said that it is ille-gal to keep any striper, regardless of size, from the Pennsylvania state line up to Trenton Falls from 1/1 through the end of February, and again from April 1st through the end of May. The fish are not feeding in the two months of Winter shown, and properly existing fear is that so-called "anglers" will try to snag those then that are in a semi-dormant stage. In the two months, April and May, the fish are spawning and surely must be left alone!

Of course if we want to stretch things a bit, we can just wander south further, past the Pennsylvania state line in Marcus Hook, where we will shortly get into Delaware Bay.

Fishermen heading out from ports in Delaware on the west, or Fortescue and Cape May on the Jersey side, have some fine fish-ing available, and while we technically are no longer in one of Pennsylvania's "50 Best," do try these waters. Weakfish, monster drum, bluefish, fluke, big stripers, etc., are all here.

#33 LEVITTOWN LAKE

Let's talk about this relatively modest little lake, one in which large stockings of trout take place. As an example, 2,700 were put in here before the 2000 season began, and in an equal number, no doubt, were added during the spring. This is an ideal facility to bring the little people to.

Bart's Tackle Shop in Tullytown has told me about this lake for several years during my outreach for information on behalf of the 'Fisherman Magazine'. I therefore turned to Bart for more specific details and he was glad to help.

Heading from north of Tullytown, Bucks County, from the Junction of US 1 and US 13, take US 13 South 4.2 miles. Pass four exits and the next one is Levittown Parkway, where you will make a right turn at the traffic light. Stay on Levittown Parkway for only 4/10 of a mile, passing two traffic lights, and turn right onto Lakeside Drive. Follow Lakeside Drive for one mile, straight into the parking area and boat ramp.

If you are coming from south of Tullytown, from the junction of US 13 and the entrance to the Pa., Turnpike's exit #29, head North on US 13 for 2.2 miles. Pass three lights and take the next exit on your right (Levittown Parkway), crossing US 13 at the light and getting onto Levittown Parkway. Travel 4/10 of a mile, passing two lights, and make a right onto Lakeside Drive. One mile later, you are at the parking lot and ramp.

Since this is a well populated area of the state, you can just imagine how crowded a "trout pond" gets. Well, in spite of heavy pounding, the lake produces plenty of fish. Just try to keep away during the warm weekend days of May.

Bart said that all boats must be registered, power or otherwise. Gas engines are not allowed, but you may use an electric kicker.

This is a Pa. Fish Commission Lake and it is listed as an Approved Trout Water — with Pa., license and trout stamp being required. As such, it's closed to fishermen from April 1st* yearly until 8:00am on Opening Day of the regular Trout Season. Reviewing my material, *Mike was good enough to point out that the lake is in the state's late winter stocking program so it's legal to fish here from March 1st to April 1st, unlike most Pa. stocked water.

Rules? We have them, but they also make sense. For example,

no overnight camping, or alcohol, or swimming — and no fires or littering. If you want any of the above, go to bigger waters.

The area is closed to the public at 10:00pm and opens again at 5:00am.

Primary targets are brown and rainbow trout, as well as the golden-orange rainbow, often called palomino.

Largemouth bass are in the lake, along with bluegills, pumpkin-seed, crappie, perch, catfish and carp.

Many of the trout are fooled with small spinners, but guys catch limits on bait more often. Every conceivable variety of bait works. A piece of chicken liver, for example, will entice lots of trout, and an occasional big catfish too.

A variety of colors of Power Bait will do the trick. Try a char-treuse nugget, pushed up the shank to the eye, and then add a few meal worms. The Power Bait floats the mealies up off bottom where the trout can easily see their next, and maybe, last meal. Go with a foot drop from your small sinker, down to a number eight bait holder hook. The Power Bait will lift the meal worm up above any low weeds present.

Bart weighed in a rainbow in the past few years that exceeded 7 pounds. So don't think these fish are just little ones. Many are a foot long or bigger, and he also told me that the largest largemouth bass he ever saw caught in the lake went a full 8 pounds!

Observe the appropriate limits and seasons, and bring a kid with you. They will have a blast!

#34 LAKE MARBURG

A "Two-story" lake, one that holds many trout along with a variety of other fish like largemouth's, northern pike, muskellunge, walleye and panfish.

Found in York County, within Codorus State Park, the lake is near Hanover, Pa (watch out, there are at least two other "Hanover's" in the state), and is crossed by Route 216.

Seven free boat ramps provide you access to all sections of the lake and since the horsepower is restricted to 10, this makes it easy to go anywhere on the lake quickly. All but one offer parking for at least ten cars. The one in Luckenbough Cove offers roadside parking only.

Area Manager Mike Kaufmann told me that the large and small-mouth bass population is excellent, ditto white perch, but walleye catches have declined. In addition to these fish, northern pike are caught as well as yellow perch with rainbow trout the salmonoid in residence. Spotfin and spottail shiners are what they find to eat.

15-23 inch rainbow trout are caught below and within the thermocline. And you will also locate excellent tail-race fishing in Codorus Creek for wild brown trout as far downstream as the village of Menges Mills. A portion of this stretch is in the Selective Harvest Program, and is listed in the Summary Booklet.

For some of the nicest rainbows you will ever see, find the thermocline (best way is to ask a local angler what level he caught 'em at yesterday), and set up on two anchors, fore and after.

Rig your slider float with a shiner at the thermocline mark, and start chumming! Yes, chum! Cut up some old dead baitfish and sprinkle them around the boat. Rainbow trout will smell and seek out what you drop over. Just like carp to floating bread, the trout will pick off the little chunks until they see your far tastier offering, and eat!

Mr. Kaufmann told the Pa. Angler and Boater that 4,200 rainbows are stocked each spring in the lake. This is done after Opening Day so that anglers are not kept off the lake until Opening Day.

These 10 inchers grow to 13½ to 15 inches later in that same fall. While rainbow trout normally grow by only ¼ inch a month, the forage here allows them to stretch out far sooner.

He said that anglers use downriggers for trout with 15-17 inchers most commonly caught.

So be it a 'bow you seek or many another species, Lake Marburg has a wide variety — and campsites too!

#35 NESHAMINY CREEK

I turned to Bobbi of Robinson's Gun and Tackle in Southampton for the real scoop about her favorite nearby waters, The

Neshaminy Creek.

Found running through much of middle and lower Bucks County in the eastern edge of Pennsylvania, the Creek eventually empties into the Delaware River.

Fish and Boat stocks trout throughout the spring in a 2 mile stretch bisected by Rt. 263, southeast of Doylestown. 3,000 were put in the Creek before Opening Day in 2,000!

An access site would be at Mill Road which crosses a nice stretch of the Creek just east of York Road over a shady old bridge. Further downstream, Dark Hollow Road turns off Almshouse Road (between Rtes 611 and 263) and dead ends at the Creek. Below the bridge are abundant carp.

Two branches meet in Rushland, just west of Rte 232, along Sacketts Ford Rd. Bobbi said that you might fish all day here along this lovely stretch and never see another angler.

The Neshaminy winds all through Tyler State Park, over two dams, with good pockets of fishing throughout. Panfish, small-mouth bass, catfish and carp are found along this beautiful part of the creek.

Parking and picnicking are plentiful in the park, and every June, local townships holds a Family Fishing Derby at the main dam in the center of the park. It is always held on the first Saturday in June, one of Pennsylvania's two "Fish-For-Free" days, when no license is required.

Playwicki County Park is accessible from Maple Avenue (Rte 213) just west of Langhorne. Brush from floods provides good shelter for largemouth bass and great fishing for the patient angler. At Hulmeville Falls, where Hulmeville Road (Rte 513) crosses the Creek, carp, large and smallmouth along with walleyes are found. The carp favor corn while the bass like medium shiners the best. Bobbi recommends fathead minnows for walleye.

The Neshaminy travels on through Newportville and Bensalem (near I-95) and this stretch is full of smallmouths, bluegills and catfish. In Croydon, the Creek widens where it meets the Delaware, bordering Neshaminy State Park. Ample parking can be found at this spot with picnic sites and playgrounds for the wee folk. As

Bobbi put it, "Where the rivers join, the muskie play and the fishing is great!" Now don't you want to just go out and try it?

#36 NOCKAMIXON STATE PARK LAKE

Big tiger muskellunge lurk in the waters of Nockamixon, as well as bucket and bronzeback bass, plus pickerel, walleye, crappie and other panfish. Oh yeah, hybrid striped bass too, my favorites. (If you promise to not tell members of The Carp Anglers Club, it holds big-scalers too — shhh). And now let's get you to it!

East of the Nockamixon Sports Shop in Quakertown, Bucks County, this 10 h. p. maximum, long and narrow lake holds many fish. Rte 563 runs to the north, and up and down its westerly side.

Take 313 in Quakertown to Rte 563 North for one way to go. Or off Rte 412, head to Rte 563 South.

Four free boat ramps offer easy access to the upper and lower ends of the lake.

Besides the fish already in residence, in 1999 Pennsylvania added chain pickerel, channel catfish, true strain and hybrid striped bass, along with walleye.

Dave Freeburger is the President of Nockamixon Sports and he was glad to share details with me about the lake.

The lake contains 1,450 acres, the park proper has picnic areas and rest rooms. His store is open 7 days a week and is only 2 miles west of the lake on Route 313.

Depths range up to 100 feet. The lake has many weed beds as well as lay down trees along the shoreline. Creek channels and rip-raps are other sure places to seek out fish.

The main forage base consists of alewife herring and gizzard shad. Fish and Boat, as well as local volunteers, have placed fish structure cribs and spawning platforms in areas of the lake that have needed structure to assist bass in spawning.

While the lake holds bigger fish, the top specimens that Freeburger has actually seen in his 18 years at the lake were bass to 7+, a 10 lb. walleye, muskie to 18, monster slab crappie heavier than 3-pounds, hybrid stripers to 15 (oh my) pounds, channel cats better'n 20, and chain pickerel of 5 pounds or more.

"Mr. Crappie" (Bill Morris) hit this 3.5 slab crappie
on a live minnow at Lake Nockamixon.

Bass of 3-5 pounds are caught quite readily in the summer at night. The lake falls under the State's Big Bass Special Regulations.

Bass lures of choice are: Spring — Rattling lipless crankbaits, spinner baits, or weighted floating plastic worms or lizards. Come summer he goes with diving crankbaits, buzzbaits early or late in the day, as well as Carolina rigged worms plus jig 'n pig's.

At night in the summer the lures to use are topwater plugs, buzzbaits, or shallow running 5-7 inch chrome plugs that are minnow shaped.

Come fall he continues with buzzbaits, jig 'n pig, as well as Carolina rigged worms.

Crappie anglers do well using fathead minnows or small maribu jigs with curlytail's.

And for walleye, a night crawler trolled on a harness along the weed edges is super, ditto live bait, or minnow plugs and curly tail jigs.

Top lures for hybrid stripers, most of which are caught at night, are large shallow running minnow plugs. By day the Rocket's want large live baits or white bucktails along 20-25 foot steep drop-offs into creek channels.

The musky plug is the typical large one, the biggest you are not ashamed to cast, ditto monster spinners along the weed beds.

Pickerel go after spoons, spinners and minnow plugs in the weeds too. If your pickerel plug is inhaled by one of their big family members, I hope you have a big net!

Channel catfish are caught on night crawlers but Dave said that cut bait, the bait that swim in the lake being far best, do very well. Fish the flats at night for channel's.

A Fisheries Management Field Report I found on the Internet said that the state tried to evaluate the success of muskellunge and tiger muskie stockings done in the 90's.

Gill nets set from 3/30 to 4/2/99 throughout the lake produced a good catch of tiger muskellunge, with 15 in all running from 29-40 inches. Also found were 64 hybrid bass to 13 pounds, a chain pickerel, one smallmouth, two black crappie, plus lots of largemouth's, walleye, and channel catfish. While the state had put true strain 'lunge in the lake before, since none were found, the result of this study said that they should concentrate on tiger's.

Fish Nockamixon, it's a lovely lake to try.

#37 SUSQUEHANNA RIVER (AREA SIX SECTION)

Remember that the Susquehanna runs through a large hunk of the middle east part of the state so, once again, we give you now a piece of it, that section that is within Area Six Manager Michael Kaufmann's domain.

The 45.25 mile part he manages runs from the York Haven Dam downstream to the Maryland state line. In our next section we will tell you about the wonderful fishing that is upstream, with heavy concentrations of smallies. Now let's get to Mr. Kaufmann's waters.

Area 6 waters of the Susquehanna flow freely from the dam — York Haven on the west and Falmouth on the east, all the way down until Route 30 crosses it at Columbia. Then it becomes a series of impoundments and tail races that are formed by the Safe Harbor, Holtwood and Conowingo Dam's.

He said that the main forage fish are a variety of minnows, plus crayfish and gizzard shad. The fish that seek them out are small-mouth bass, channel and white catfish, with walleye from one end to the other. Down at the Conowingo Dam Pool he said that large-mouth bass are in residence. (I have fished this stretch and caught both largemouth bass on night crawlers and carp on corn kernels). Mr. Kaufmann wrote to ask me to let you know that large carp are present throughout the free flowing and impounded stretches of the river.

A recent stocking of true strain striped bass occurred in Lancaster County, providing winter fishing at Peach Bottom Atomic Power Plant and summer fishing in the vicinity of the Holtwood Dam tailrace and Rte. 372 bridge.

Stripers also went into York County along with true strain and tiger muskies, plus walleye.

The York Haven Dam is found in the northern tip of Lancaster County at Falmouth, and an unlimited horsepower boat ramp is here in the York Haven tail race.

Heading south, next comes the public ramp at Marietta, and then Columbia, each in Lancaster County. Continuing down, we reach the Safe Harbor Dam pool's upper end where a ramp is in Wrightsville, York County. Same County, is Long Level, off Rte 624, on the west side of the river, owned by PP&L Power, in the Safe Harbor Pool itself. Now on the east side of the river, we get to Pequea in Lancaster County, at the upper end of the Holtwood Dam's Pool. Further, we get to Muddy Creek, below Rte 372 in York County, at upper end of the Conowingo Dam's Pool. And in the Conowingo Dam Pool itself we get to the Peach Bottom Atomic Plant ramp with access provided by PECO Energy.

These very clear directions should allow you to seek out the wide variety of fish that are in the Susky.

Average air temperatures in this area are warmer than in much of the state, allowing you to fish a longer bass season. Remember though that the river takes a lot of boat pounding because it is so very good.

Honorable Mention: Well we can't forget Chambers Lake in Hybernia County Park, Chester County. A Fish and Boat Field Report showed that, especially since the lake was only opened on 6/12/99 to angling, it has many fish of good size. Chain pickerel and largemouth bass were the kings of the lake.

Also found were a wide variety of perch and sunnies, with crappie too, and channel catfish have been stocked, ditto tiger muskies and golden shiners to feed them all.

Manager Kaufmann likes Codurus Creek which we told you above flows out of Lake Marburg — a Selective Harvest stretch is on the creek for the resident Wild Brownies.

Many a young person has caught her/his first trout at Lake Luxemburg (within Core Creek Park) in Middletown Township, Bucks County so we must include it in our close-to-best spots. In fact, Wayne Martin contacted me with some useful information about it.

He said that the lake itself is 156 acres, with four fishing piers, a regular boat ramp (electric only), and another crude one for canoes. A very modest fee is charged annually for use of the ramp/s.

Wayne reported a maximum depth of 18 feet in the center of the lake with sharp drop-offs from shore. Man-made in the 70's, plenty of open bank space exists.

Trout are the main target and for bait, Power Bait in fluorescent orange and chartreuse is best. Martin also gets bass, walleye, catfish, and carp here too.

And one day, maybe in the next book, we will increase the "best" tally to 60 — if so, the Schuykill may make the list. The river runs right through Philadelphia and contains oodles of smallmouth bass, plus largemouth's and tiger muskies.

CHAPTER 7

Area Seven

T he area defined as #7 encompasses parts of 20 counties in all, a vast amount of territory indeed. The entire lower middle part of the state is in this Area, including Blair to its northwest, to part of Schuykill to the east. And over to the southwest it involves a small piece of Somerset, ranging across the southern tier of Pennsylvania over to York County.

In all, we are talking about a great range of water, and for help, I wrote to Area Manager Lawrence Jackson. He turned me over to his Fisheries Technician, Timothy Wilson and later, reviewed my material for me!

#38 CANOE LAKE

I don't know about you, but I never heard about Canoe Lake until Tim wrote to me. What I can tell you though, based on my research, is that, if I am ever anywhere near Altoona, I might just drive east a bit to Frankstown in the northwestern part of Area 7, Blair County. Canoe Lake can be reached via U. S. Highway #22.

Canoe Lake is in Canoe Creek State Park, and is managed under several Special Regulations, so check out the Summary before fishing it. As we went to print, it was a Late Winter Trout and Big Bass lake.

*Here's a typical Area 7 largemouth and no —
it wasn't caught in Indiana.*

The lake covers 155 acres and contains three boat ramps. Docks are here as well and the really good news is that Canoe Lake is very angler-friendly. 96% of the shoreline is available to shore anglers. You may fish from your boat here via arm power or electric motor only.

Known for its good trout fishing, Canoe also holds a wide variety of warm water fish as well.

The pre-season stocking of trout at Canoe in 2000 was very impressive, with 7,000 trout in all being put into the lake. During the year, of course, thousands more were added. Nearby Canoe Creek also received 2,500 trout before the Opening Day of 2000, by the way.

Muskellunge and walleye were stocked here in 1999, fingerling sized too, not just "fry."

Besides trout, other species includes good populations of large-mouth bass, panfish and chain pickerel. Of course another member of the pickerel clan, its big cousin, muskellunge, is the king of the lake, and as pointed out in the above paragraph, the state is serious about establishing Canoe as muskie water, adding still more often. Walleye are another fish that comes from the lake.

Mr. Wilson also pointed out that the park offers plenty of parking and has walking trails to all parts of the lake.

Between the serenity that an Electric Motor only lake can provide, and the rest of the material we just gave you, I hope you will agree that this sounds like a great spot to fish for both peace and quiet, with some fine fishing thrown in to boot!

#39 CONEWAGO (PINCHOT) LAKE

Tricky, this one, because it has two different names. First let's find the southeast tip of Area 7, in northern York County, and then head to Gifford Pinchot State Park to reach the lake.

The best access roads are to the west off of I-83 or from US-15 at Dillsburg, head east via PA-74 and PA-177.

The Atlas shows the lake as Pinchot (Conewago), but let's still call it Conewago because that appears to be the name that the state prefers to use. If you are in Rossville though, the closest town, ask for directions to Pinchot because that is what the local's call it.

The list of fish stocked into the lake in one year alone included channel catfish, muskellunge, walleye, and white x striped bass. This last fish is the one that you have already seen me call "Rocket," and it is the same critter that southern anglers call "Sunshine" bass.

To be found swimming in Conewago are the above foursome, along with a variety of panfish, plus lots of largemouth bass and a handful of smallies.

The lake falls under Big Bass regulations so if you are after a bass for a meal, make sure it falls within the season and special size limit called for in the Summary.

In the Jan/Feb. 1999 issue of Pa. Angler and Boater Area Manager Jackson reported that the regulation, in place since 1987,

*Here's a typical largemouth caught at Conewago/Pinchot
by Eric Becker.*

resulted in excellent survey results in May, 1998. The heaviest
bass found then was a 6-pounder and 12-18 inchers were abundant.

Four access points are provided in the park for boaters, even
though the lake only contains 350 acres. Electric-motor only

restrictions are in place but in a body of water so relatively small, you really don't need a lot of giddyap to reach your target area.

Larry Jackson pointed out that adequate parking is available at each ramp. Three also have docks, and each site allows you to fish from shore.

Another fisherman-friendly lake, 95% of the lakes shoreline is available to anglers.

Mr. Wilson told us that the lake contains an excellent fishery for largemouth bass. Featured too are good populations of black crappie, channel catfish and other panfish. He added that the lake also contains walleye, hybrid (YES!) striped bass, and muskellunge fisheries that "can provide an exciting surprise to the average angler."

You "sissy-bass" (largemouth's for the uninformed) fishermen will find that a hybrid bass weighing three pounds can tow your 6 pound bucketmouth behind it and not lose a stroke. Therefore, if you are on this lake, make sure you are fishing an open drag because one bite from a hybrid may very well result in the breaking of your line. A 5 pound "Rocket" can easily snap your rod too if you are using heavy line so, have some respect, willya?

#40 JUNIATA RIVER

We will talk to you later on in this Area about Raystown Lake, the still water in Area 7 that gets the heaviest pressure. The Raystown Branch of the Juniata originates in Allegheny Township, Somerset County, then flows through Bedford County, and then goes into Raystown Lake itself. It comes back out again for five miles as the Raystown Branch, and then into the Juniata River proper. The River runs another 80 or so miles and then drops out into the Susquehanna.

I suppose that if you drove concentric circles within south central Pennsylvania, you will eventually reach a part of the Juniata. It can also be found in Mifflin, Juniata, Perry, Blair and Huntington Counties as well.

Some access points to the lower river will be off Route 915, or further down, along Route 26 at Warriors Path State Park where you can find a launch ramp.

Years back, well known writer Jim Bashline wrote an article in Field and Stream which called the Juniata River "one of the best kept secrets in the world of fishing."

Bashline simply loved the Juniata for its excellent smallmouth bass fishing. He said that it is not too deep or fast, making it wader friendly. His favorite area was off US 322/22 between Lewistown and Mifflintown. He pointed out that a float trip might be the best style of all to cover the river. He liked to catch smallies on any kind of crawfish lookalike, but also hit them on surface stuff.

Fish and Boat surveyed the river in the stretch from Lewistown and Millerstown during 17 nights in April and early May in 1999. They found 782 smallies alone that were a foot long or better with the biggest measuring in excess of 21 inches! No wonder he liked it for smallies.

Bashline also liked the river for muskellunge. In the 5/16/2000 report of stockings I received from Fish and Boat, it showed 11 separate stockings of muskies took place that year in four counties. As with lake trout, the favorite food for 'lunge are suckers so if you can get a six-eight incher, try it on, or else a matching plug.

In that Spring '99 survey we discussed, Fish and Boat found several muskies from as little as 10 inches up to 46 inches long.

Add to these two, a fine population of walleye, and you have the threesome that got most of Jim's attention on the Juniata. 152 walleye were electrofished during the above samplings and the longest taped out at 26.5 inches.

The state put walleye into Huntington County's part of the river four times one year and three more at Mifflin County to expand that fishery even further.

Anglers who drift downstream often do the best for 'eye's, casting jig and live bait combo's. Some (like the lazy angler who wrote this book), prefer to anchor, but folks who drift and control their retrieve certainly cover more water and often catch more walleye.

And if you want action, the number one inhabitant of the Juniata River is rockbass so if you would like some good eating panfish, go light with worms and catch a limit!

A surprising number of brown trout were found in the Lewistown to Millerstown stretch with several being very large. It was assumed that the trout would return to colder tributaries once the river warmed up.

Several large channel catfish and big carp too were noted by the state in that sampling.

Writer and top photographer Vic Attardo said that the rock strata that forms the base of the Juniata River provides cover for the flow's sizable population of smallmouth bass, as well as an interesting challenge to the angler fishing the river.

Along great portions of the river, the strata consists of irregular ledges that run nearly perpendicular to the current. These ledges, which resemble corrugated cardboard, are a compressed series of raised bands and depressions. The structure extends out to meet the main channel, or in some places, runs across the width of the river.

Smallmouth hold to these ledges in two ways. Frequently, they'll establish themselves in the dips within the ledges; in other places, they'll lurk near the channel where a ledge meets deep water.

Successful presentation of a fly, lure or bait requires the angler be aware of the river bottom and how the smallmouth are positioned. Within the ledges, bass usually face upstream into the current, just like trout in moving water. However, it is not unusual for smallmouth to orientate themselves downstream, if the current swirls back over a ledge.

Typically, smallmouth will lie at the bottom of a depression within the corrugated ridges, and also off the main channel where the ledge meets deeper water. Whatever the fisherman throws, it should be allowed to drift into the depressions as well as the drop-offs where a ledge meets the channel.

Cast across or slightly downstream so that your offering travels sideways with the current. Let it ride over the peaks in the ledge, then fall into the dips behind the peaks. Look for depressions where the water appears greener or darker than the surrounding water. This is often the home of the biggest bass in the area!

I'm sorry to be so dis-jointed in reporting to you about this river,

*Creek-Guide Shane Bender of Kish Creek Outfitters
sent me this photo of an 18 inch wild brownie caught
(and released) on a Sulphur nymph.*

but if you try to follow its strange meanderings through its long path you will realize that it covers so much range that it was a tough task to write about. I counted 19 sites in all that offer access to the public when I scoured the free map I got from Fish and Boat. Repeated elsewhere in the book, let me again remind you to contact the Pennsylvania Fish and Boat folks for a copy of it.

#41 KISHACOQUILLAS CREEK ("KISH")

And if you got the spelling right without any help, get to the head of the class! 7,600 trout were stocked into four sections of "Kish" Creek before Opening Day of 2000 and three stretches were "sweetened" too during the season. So if you are looking for a fine place to catch trout, head to Mifflin County and look up this site.

You will remember that I told you about the outreach I did for help to stores that sell fishing licenses. Well, one store that replied was Kish Creek Outfitters in Burnham, and to owner/guide Shane Bender, my sincere thanks for all his assistance. And obviously, if you want to hit "Kish" Creek, check him out!

Kish Creek meanders through Kishacoquillas Valley, south of Route 655, and hooks south east at Lumber City, running down Route 322 until it enters into the site we just discussed, The Juniata!

In addition to the 7,600 rainbow and brown trout that were stocked pre-season, and the in-season additions made, Shane said that the creek has plenty of Wild brown trout available too.

Take Route 322 west headed to State College off the Lewiston exit to reach his favorite beat. Bender feels that some of the best fishing can be found from the Walnut Street Bridge down to the mouth of the Juniata River.

In fact, on the Juniata, Bender fishes from the mouth of Kish Creek up to the railroad bridge in Granville near the Locust Camp Ground. He suggests hitting it at this spot with the largest stone catfish you can get as bait to catch some of the biggest smallmouth bass and walleye.

But back to "Kish," the top fishing occurs between mid-April and late fall. Fly fishermen do best from early in May until the early part of June. The stream offers one of the best Sulphur hatches in the whole state.

If you are a bait fisherman, go with minnows, spinners or Power Baits. If the creek is high and discolored, use a baby night crawler and bounce it down current. try using a miniature marshmallow at the eye of the hook to allow the worm to ride a bit high in the current to make it easier for the trout to both see and eat!

#42 RAYSTOWN LAKE

Bass, three kinds! Smallmouth, largemouth, and stripers, all are in Raystown, as well as a variety of other fine fish!

Far and away the largest body of non-moving water in Area 7, Raystown is in Huntington County, and dumps out into the Raystown Branch of the Junita River.

The lake proper offers nine public access sites. They all charge an entry fee but you will probably find that it was money worth spending. They all permit unlimited horsepower and each has a dock as well as parking for at least 10 cars.

Only the Seven Points Marina, a private facility, does not allow shore fishing. All the other facilities have plenty of "standing room." In fact, the site named Aitch, situated on the west side of the center of the lake, near Marklesburg, even has a fishing pier.

Route 22 heads over the top of the lake at Huntington, and Route 26 runs down its entire westerly side. From the south, take 70/76 to Route 26 and hook north to the lake.

Tiger muskies and muskellunge are in Raystown, competing with walleye and trout as well as the above noted bass for the ample supply of bait.

The stocking list I received showed that true strain striped bass (100,000 one year) were put here. That same year 8,300 small tiger muskellunge went in. The 50,000 small lake trout put in were longer than the other two to allow for growth and a chance at escape too. They are not as fast as some other fish so size alone often means life.

Area 7 Fisheries Manager Jackson said that, even though Raystown is hardly underexploited, it holds a good population of walleyes that anglers have not been able to master. I suppose that the main answer to this puzzle would come from night fishing but those who do it don't talk!

A Field & Stream article in 2/99 told us that landlocked striped bass grow very large at Raystown. The article pointed to the 53¾ pound striper caught in 1994 by Robert Price as an example.

Fisheries Technician Brian Chikotas was quoted as saying that "there's a huge forage base of gizzard shad and alewives" with stripers stocked in the lake reaching 20 inches by the end of their third year in the water.

The lake covers 8,300 acres as it wanders like a snake through its many twists and turns. F&S quoted Nick Lambert, then President of the Raystown Striper Club, as saying that the peak catches occur in mid-spring into June and, based on temperatures, sometimes into early July.

Lambert told the F&S reporter that the style of choice involves trolling large white bucktail streamers 18-20 feet down off of downriggers. Just make sure your snap isn't on too tight or else that big "rock" will certainly break your line with ease.

As summer approaches, the striped bass don't stop eating, they simply change their eating pattern. As with walleye, the time to fish for both is in the dark of night. Stripers offshore or walleye in, both are there for the taking.

A 34-pound striper was pictured in the March/April 2000 issue of Pa. Angler and Boater, taken in Raystown by William B. Lawton who was using live bait in July — and on only 12 pound test line!

And if you want to read a wonderful story about "Old Rubber Lips" (carp), get that same issue if you can and look on page 35 to see a superb contest winning entry. Dale Hartman wrote about a 19 pound carp he caught and released one day way back when at Seven Points.

Not at the Marina, but just a bit north of it on the west side is Seven Points and here is where Mr. Hartman told his story of striper fishing with two friends as well as tackling carp.
Back in 1999, Fish and Boat reported on the Internet that gillnettings done that April showed 16 species of fish captured in their 14 net sites, between Weaver's Falls and the dam.

The biggest fish found were striped bass up to 33.5 pounds, lake trout to 30 inches, and a tiger muskie that weighed 17.2 pounds. Add smallies to 21+ inches and channel catfish to 26 and you have a most impressive list indeed. However, now throw in the most commonly found fish, walleyes, with 106 of them making legal size, up to 9.3 pounds and you know that Raystown has both big and lots of fine fish.

The nettings done in 1999 showed higher catches than three prior surveys taken between 1983 and 1994. And since walleye were proven to be both reproducing and also quite numerous in

Raystown, stocking of them were to have been stopped. However, the other fish talked about above will continue to be stocked.

Here's a tip for those who like to catch fish, during the day. That's during the absolute middle of the day, not at a time that you either have to stumble out so early that you are walking in the dark, or get back home in the dark at the other end of the day.

Think lake trout! Simple, lakers feed all day long, and the deepest water will be the best place to fish. If boat traffic is not severe, and it generally isn't other than in the summer, try double-anchor fishing.

Fish bottom with both your rods but if you want to fish one up high for stripers, etc., go for it. Just remember that lakers are kind of lazy. Alewives will fool most fish, and in fact, are number one on their diet, but I far prefer to use a large golden shiner, talked about previously, with my sinker on bottom and the bait fish swimming freely on a three foot leader.

Please do remember that if you do not want to take your laker home, reel it up very slowly so that you don't give it the bends. If their stomach expands during the ride up, chances are slim to none that they can return to the bottom. Know too that lakers generally spawn in lakes during the period between mid-September and late November so read your Summary to make sure that it is legal to take one home when you catch it.

#43 SUSQUEHANNA RIVER — AREA 7

Excuse me for repeating myself, but once again, the Susquehanna covers so very much territory that it is impossible to give you a very good and full picture in this book. Therefore, if you want to check out the river, all of it, with its various limbs, buy the separate book about it. You will probably read that it is the best smallmouth water in the whole east.

Of course don't tell that to my fellow author, Joe Kasper, who will argue with you tooth and nail that The Delaware River is better, and since he has written a few books about "The Big D," he is not one to try and convince that the Susquehanna is better than his river.

Happy angler Frank Foley took this big smallmouth bass at the Area 7 stretch of the Susquehanna River in November of 1999.

The Area 7 section has the Juniata River entering the Susquehanna at State Access Site #652 in Perry County — called Riverfront Campground and Rent A Boat. Mr. Jackson's territory runs clear south, through several other counties, including Dauphin, past Harrisburg to the east, and down to the point where the river comes under the jurisdiction of Area Manager Kaufmann back in Area 6.

Relatively new regulations for smallmouth bass will help, but in the Pennsylvania Angler and Boater, Manager Jackson said that he feels that habitat alone makes the river wonderful for bronzebacks, tied in with so many an angler who practices Catch and Release!

He said that exceptional smallmouth fishing exists around Harrisburg, Duncannon and Marysville, where rock outcrops and rocky shelves offer hiding place a'plenty. The river is as wide as a mile in some of this section and is also quite shallow, making for excellent wading, he added.

We have already referred to Vic Attardo, photographer extraordinaire, and writer. In the last edition of the year 1999 he wrote for Angler and Boater that fall fishing on the Susky can be the best time of the year, because it doesn't cost him a lot of lost sleep. (Well, my interpretation anyway of his words). As days get shorter, he fishes the river later in the morning than during the earlier times of the year.

He fishes jigs, very slowly, in the river early each fall, noting that it is critical to cast away from the boat and retrieve your jig very, very slowly. Attardo points out that these fish are very spooky and that any fish that you pass over will pass by your lure. Spinnerbaits will do the trick too but a slipbobber with live bait is generally the best way to fish as the water gets too cold for smallies to chase a lure.

I had the opportunity of meeting with Bruce at Brinkman's in Philadelphia in the summer I put my notes together for this book and besides talking about the nearby stretches of the Delaware, he helped with data about Area 7's Susky.

Bruce has a customer who fishes out of the campground we first referred to up above, Riverfront. They can be contacted for details at 1-717-834-5252. Remember, this is where the river is met by the Juniata.

He said that 50+ smallmouth days are quite common in this area and that the folks who run the camp will not only rent a canoe to you for float trips, but can also take you up to your starting point and pick you back up when you are done. Chances are you will really be "done" by then and in need of help if you get into the kind of fishing I was told about. The Campground can be found at Duncannon, below Benvenue. In a two day float trip in 2000, a pair of Brinkman's customers nearly went nuts, catching 80 or more smallies daily to 4 pounds.

Remember that a Closed Season exists as well as Big Bass regulations. Things change, but when I wrote this book it was open from the third Saturday in June until the last day in February.

In cold water, Bruce said the way to go is with live bait. While anglers generally go with small fish, he prefers crawfish, leeches, and helgrammites, in that order. And instead of fallfish (chub), he likes killies even more.

As the water warms and the smallmouth population gets more active he prefers using ⅛ to ¼ ounce tube jigs. Pumpkin seed and motor oil, plus smoke colors, are the best colors.

The river also contains walleye and both kinds of muskies. In fact, in the Dauphin County portion in 1999, fingerling muskies were stocked twice, tiger's once, and walleye fry were released three times. Add muskies and walleye in Juniata County, still more of each in Northumberland, again in Perry, on down to York County where Area 7 meets Area 6. In this stretch, they also put true-strain striped bass and tigers.

Brinkman's Bruce told me that when you get further south, more largemouth bass join the smallies. And you certainly know that lowly (hah!) carp are in the river as well as suckers and fallfish.

The Susquehanna? Oh yes! Just remember that it can very mean. Just ask the residents of Wilkes-Barre up in Area 4. They have been flooded several times, so exercise extreme caution on the river if it is on the rise, please!

#44 YELLOW BREECHES CREEK

And for the last of our 50 Best in Area 7, let's go trout fishing again. Yellow Breeches Creek is situated in Cumberland County and while best known for trout, the Atlas also said it has panfish plus large and smallmouth bass.

Area 7 Fisheries Technician Tim Wilson suggested my including

Yellow Breeches was where Jim Slinsky
caught this good sized brownie.

the Creek in our list and I agree!

The Creek provides 43 miles of trout fishing in Cumberland County, from the bridge on PA233 all the way to the mouth in New Cumberland at the Susquehanna.

Access is available along PA 174 and PA 114. It is south of US 81 and State Road 233 runs through its upper-section.

Of special note is the Catch and Release — Artificial Lures Only section near Boiling Springs.

The Creek is stocked with brook, brown and rainbow trout. An incredible 20,150 in all were put into the Creek before the season started in 2000 and a similar amount went in during the year.

If you are looking for a fly that works as well as or better than most, all year long, go with a terrestrial in Yellow Breeches. Try an ant in size 18 or so and you will probably see it sucked in shortly.

Trout? Yellow Breeches, and even if you are not in the Catch and Release section, that doesn't mean that you have to take them home.

And for Honorable Mention, there are really several to tell you about in Area 7. For example, down in southern Bedford County, not far from the border with Maryland, are Koon and Gordon Lakes. They are both owned by the Evitts Creek Water Company and electric motor powered boats were recently added to those that can fish the lake.

The lakes provide water to the City of Cumberland, Maryland, and officials from both states cooperated to make these spots available to anglers.

A recent survey showed Koon (268 acres) and Gordon (120) to both contain lots of panfish. So bring the can of worms and a child and show them how to do it.

Shawnee Lake, also in Bedford County, is worth mention too. It's 451 acres were surveyed in April of 1999 and the population found was remarkable. Drawdown from 95-96, only a few years later, it held more and bigger pike than before the drawdown, and many other fish too. Try it!

CHAPTER 8

Area Eight

L ast but far from least is the southwestern part of the state, wherein we find Area Fisheries Manager Richard Lorson in control. Rick supplied us with quite a bit of useful material, both directly, and through an interview he had with the Pa. Angler and Boater in its first issue of 1999.

Area 8 consists of all or parts of ten counties, from Beaver to Cambria on its upper side, down to Greene across to Somerset. Within this section a lot of fine fishing exists, as well as extremely dense population in and around Pittsburgh. In the Pittsburgh area, three hot rivers flow and join. They are the Allegheny, the Monongahela and the Ohio, and super action takes place in all! Read on:

#45 THE ALLEGHENY RIVER (LOWER)

Rick Lorson manages the Allegheny from the point it enters Pittsburgh back up northeast to Clinton, Pa., (there's a few "Clintons," but this stretch is found in Allegheny and Armstrong Counties).

Going back to studies made by the Commission in the mid-90's, 47 varieties of fish in all were found in different sections of the river! They range from shorthead redhorse to walleye. Also from

*Here's the kind of walleye they catch
in the lower Allegheny River.*

logperch to log length carp, and in between, lots of other critters.

Recommendations to the Commission included continued efforts toward improving water quality and habitat protection. Further, attention to be given to manage the fishery for reproducing smallmouth bass, walleye, sauger, rock bass, white bass, channel catfish, and carp.

The report also included annual planting of muskies, or tiger muskies above. The lower part of the Allegheny, closest to its juncture with the "Mon" and Ohio, both of whom get hybrid stripers, to get this wonderful species as well.

Big bass rules were recommended to improve smallmouth bass catches and sizes.

The lower Allegheny covers a 72 mile stretch, including the very busy waters around Pittsburgh, as well as the peace and quiet found at Brady's Bend. An article in the 2/2000 edition of Pa. Angler and Boater told us that the Army Corp of Engineers has eight lock-and-dam systems on the river, with long and narrows pools. Each pool is between two dams and the main purpose of the dams is to permit commercial barge traffic to flow smoothly.

If you want some of the best action around, fish these pools when the boat traffic is at its lightest, of course.

Whatever you do, don't get in the way of a barge being towed or pushed. Control is non-existent, so keep away.

Strong 1993 and 1995 year classes were found on the river for walleye, sauger and smallies. They also found 9-14 inch white bass in goodly numbers in the Spring of 1998.

As noted above, muskies and tiger muskies have made their presence known on the lower river. Since the river holds emerald shiners galore, try using the biggest ones you can for the Green Giants. Some favor suckers, but here in the darker waters, we suggest the brilliant emerald with its shiny stripe running from gill to tail.

The waters of Allegheny County received stockings of true strain and tiger muskellunge in 1999 along with hybrid bass as well as paddlefish too. As already said, both muskies were put above in Armstrong County that year, with lots of fry sized walleye as well as more paddlefish.

If you add up the walleye that were stocked into the upper (Area 2) and lower Allegheny, one recent year, you will get a nearly unbelievable total of 11,533,000 little "fry" that were dropped in from one end to the other.

Going again to our favorite source of information, the Pennsylvania Angler & Boater, in its July/August issue of 1999 writer Jeff Knapp told us how to catch walleye in warmer water. Now everyone knows how to do it in the winter.

Just take two crazy pills, throw on all the clothing you own, bring a buddy for safety, and go out at night in a bitter snow storm. You can almost be certain of a good walleye catch. You also might be assured of a really fine trip to the nut ward if someone sees you out there.

So if creature comfort is a consideration, go in warmer times. I fished for walleye a total of seven times in a row between the end of the summer of 1999 and the start of November. Then two more times late in the spring of 2000 and in those nine outing, caught at least one walleye every time, as well as a variety of other fish. All these trips were during the day — not early or late, by the way!

Night trolling will work in warm times, with lures being pulled that imitate the young of the year shad that are falling downstream.

Boat access points can be found up and down the river. A few that are both Fish and Boat "free" launches, as well as ones that can accommodate at least ten cars are:

First in Armstrong County, #352 — "Rosstron" — at Pool 6, #355, "Cowanshannock" — Pool 7, and #356 — "Templeton," by Pool 8. Further down, in Allegheny County, look for #412, "Springdale," "Tarentum," and #417, "Deer Creek."

Knapp favors fishing shallower water for the biggest walleye. Look for readings of bait on your scope before setting up a trolling pattern and make your most serious attempts at producing fish while running upstream with your stickbaits. As you reach what you feel may be the end of a hot piece of water, don't troll back down but instead, run down and start to troll back up again.

Pull your lures through fast water in the summer, because the better oxygenated portions are more comfortable to the walleye as well as to the bait they are feeding on.

So what's your pleasure? Walleye? A million of 'em were put in and they naturally reproduce. Muskies, true and hybrid, plenty. Smallmouth bass, certainly, and don't forget sauger. And of course if "Rocket" (hybrid) bass are your thing, go get 'em here, as well as the smaller family member, white bass, the male of which being the proud father of the hybrid bass once mixed with a lady striper.

#46 THE MONONGAHELA RIVER

Remember that we are not here to talk about pollution and its long range effects. Suffice it to say that the waters in and around the busy City of Pittsburgh are not "Love Canal," but neither are they the purest of pure. So let's get back to The Summary of Fishing Regulations and Laws before you set foot on the shores of "The Mon" if you are out to catch a meal. No, the fish don't have skulls and crossbones on them, and no doubt, most are quite safe, but please err on the side of caution, okay?

Fellow Carper Bill Devine fishes The Monongahela often since he lives in Pittsburgh, but his range is far wide too so don't think he fishes here because it is close to home. He wets lines in "The Mon" because it is a "vastly underused fishery!"

Smallmouth bass, walleye, muskies, catfish, sauger, bluegill, sheepshead (A McKeesport anglerette caught a 12½ pounder here in 1999) and carp are all found in the river. Mr. Devine told me that there are hundreds of easily accessible areas to both shoreline and boat anglers within the city limits alone.

Devine likes the many lock and dam sections, as close to the bridge supports as you can get. As a strictly shore angler, he recommends fishing from anywhere in Point State Park at the confluence of the three rivers.

On the southern edge of Pittsburgh you will find the Monongahela Parking Wharf which gives anglers access to a wide variety of fish and even allows free parking on the weekends!

Just off 18th and Carson, below the Birmingham Bridge, still more shore casters can be found, as well as a free boat ramp.

Head south about a ½ hour from Pittsburgh to Elizabeth on State Road #51 and you will reach yet one more free ramp and shore fishing access.

Nearby you will find the Elizabeth Waterfront Park, where an old coal barge filled with cement offers excellent shore fishing. Bill loves this spot for smallies.

Right close by is Lock and Dam #3. Just below it is excellent catfishing. Devine witnessed a boat angler who caught a catfish on a large shiner fished at bottom. The weight? How about 40 pounds or so? Wow!

Sauger fishermen love to go after their prey on the Monongahela because it holds so many and doesn't get near the pressure you would imagine.

Six lock and dam systems run through The Mon and each presents anglers with a chance at catching quite a few bigger sauger, with more large fish than the Allegheny and Ohio Rivers.

As with their bigger family members, walleye, nothing beats a jig and live bait. While most anglers like to drift, try doing this from an anchored boat instead. Cast across the current and as the jig makes its first bump or two before rising up off bottom, this is where most of your strikes will occur.

#47 NORTH PARK LAKE/PINE CREEK

Here's a "sleeper" from a local "ringer," our friend John McKean of nearby Glenshaw.

North Park Lake is far better known for trout than anything else, but McKean said it is a fine site for many other fish. In fact, a brief noting of it as a bass, panfish, and stocked trout lake came from none other than Area Manager Rick Lorson in 1999.

Situated in Allegheny County, about 15 miles above downtown Pittsburgh, you can find it close to the town of McCandless. For better sighting, look for the lake between Ingomar, Gibsonia and Allison Park.

As John wrote, it's heavily stocked with trout but unknown to most is the fabulous big channel catfishing it offers as well as carp. Few anglers try the lake after Opening Day but that's all right with

John — he waits and then fishes for bass, panfish, carp and Mr. Whiskers once the one day a year anglers disappear.

North Park Lake flows out into Pine Creek, which has scads of carp hidden in its pools, especially as it gets closer to its juncture with the Allegheny River! Pine Creek is stocked with catchable trout and also has a Delayed Harvest Trout Regulation Area.

And for folks that want big green fish, the lake has also been stocked with tiger muskies and walleye!

The preseason stocking list for 2000 showed 6,700 trout put into its 74 acres with in season additions also. 6,000 more were added into Pine Creek before the opening gun.

So — want put 'n take trout? Plenty are in North Park, but also available are a variety of critters that can eat your trout, — some that will break your line with ease.

#48 RACCOON LAKE

Number one on the list of "Best" waters given to me in his area by Rick Lorson was this relatively small lake. You can find it in Raccoon Creek State Park, in lower Beaver County, not far from the border with West Virginia. It's 28 miles west of Pittsburgh, and 20 miles south of Beaver, near Frankfort Springs and roads that are close by are Route 168 and 18.

You can launch a small electric motor operated boat from its ramp at its east end, or fish from shore. Either way, the 101 acre lake provides trout anglers and warmwater fishermen with a wide variety of species to seek.

Well stocked with trout (it got 3,750 before Opening Day of 2000 as well as in-season plantings), you can catch them along with an assortment of other fish.

The lake is on the list to get trout in the winter, spring and fall to allow anglers nearly a year-round trout spot.

2,000 saugeye (the hybrid of walleye and sauger) went in in 1999, and Fish & Boat also placed channel catfish and walleye in the lake that year.

According to a study made in the mid-90's (and Rick was actually one of the people who performed it), "Raccoon Lake contained the best white crappie fishery in the southwest" — That should mean that crappie lovers need to mark this site down on their places to go to list.

Well, a dam control gate malfunction that fall created a need to completely draw-down the lake, so things had to be started all over again thereafter. Chances are the slab's are back again in good numbers by now though.

Maximum depth here is nearly 30 feet and the lake offers nearly 100% shoreline access other than at the dam breast and the public beach. Besides your own boat, you can also rent small boats or canoes.

After the lake was refilled in 1996, significant stockings took place, besides the ones already discussed. 2,000 fingerling channel cat's went in and maintenance stockings are expected to continue yearly. Ditto walleye — 1,000 were added after the fill, and even a supply of 300 tiger muskellunge became residents, with expected additions annually. Saugeye, in particular, as we already talked about, are a fish that the state wants to really establish here — 3,000 were placed in the lake early on.

An attempt was also made to recreate a largemouth bass fishery in the lake. Before the big draw-down it held quite a few. The first re-stocking involved 100 adult bass and 3,550 fingerlings.

Well, that gives us yet another spot that is both close to big cities, but also offers the peace and quiet that only an electric-motor restriction can provide.

If you are angling for a few trout to take home, try catching them on a piece of liver. While it is not as exciting as lure fishing, trout simply love to eat liver, preferably chicken liver — and a 5 pound channel catfish might be the creature you wind up catching instead!

Be it trout, crappie, channel catfish, or saugeye, don't forget to visit Raccoon Lake for a fun day on the water.

#49 YELLOW CREEK LAKE

Here's another of Rick Lorson's "Best" spots. The lake is in Yellow Creek State Park, Indiana County, at the top part of his territory. It's near the towns of Pikes Peak and Nolo, approximately 10 miles southeast of Indiana, Pa.

Route 422 runs over the northeast corner of the lake and 259 goes up to its back door from the south.

I found three boat ramps here on my Fishing and Boating map. All three are within the park proper and each restricts your engine to 10 horsepower. Shore anglers can fish nearby and each spot has room for at least 10 cars.

The lake is on the state's list of Big Bass waters so expect to find some big lunkers here (both largemouth and smallmouth). And yearly stockings of muskellunge and walleye occur too. Stockings of walleye fry were of enormous numbers during the mid-90's, with close to 5,000,000 wee fish going in over a four year span. Of course the overwhelming majority either died quickly or were eaten by other fish but this should tell you how serious an attempt Fish and Boat makes. It is now stocked with fingerling walleye which makes a better yet walleye fishery.

Since "Big Bass" rules apply, and since big bass like big baits, try catching a few golden shiners on a #10 hook, baited with a speck of dough or a kernel or two of corn.

Down Florida way, they call these "Wild Shiners" and they make the best bait known for the biggest bass of all. Just remember that if you are out to put 'em back, and a bass swallows the hook, cut your line rather than trying to dig the steel out. Don't use "stainless" hooks and the lunker will stand a wonderful chance at surviving a long time. The hook will rust out but meanwhile, the fish can still eat.

Rick participated in a study of the lake in 1996 and it showed that the 1991 changeover to Big Bass rules improved the bass population at the lake.

722 acres in size, a study of anglers feelings about the fishing at Yellow Creek Lake showed that 86% of them both favored the Big Bass rules, and, not surprisingly, found fishing for bass to be quite good.

The lake also has some smallmouth bass, with a great deal of panfish. The majority consisting of bluegills, pumpkinseeds, yellow perch, and brown bullhead, with black crappie too.

Very much a bass lake, the state placed felled trees, porcupine brush cribs and separate nesting and nursery areas in the lake to assist in natural reproduction.

Try those "wild shiners" you catch yourself as bait, but if a muskie grabs it, get ready to tussle with a beast.

#50 YOUGHIOGENY RIVER AND LAKE

Last but far from least on my list of the "50 Best" is this big piece of water. It starts as the Youghiogeny River to the north and becomes dammed up water south of Route 523. Route 40 runs across the lake at Somerfield and the waters are in both Fayette and Somerset Counties. The lake leaves Pennsylvania and continues into Garrett County, Maryland, so be warned that special regulations exist as a result.

The river itself flows north towards Allegheny County, after flowing through Westmoreland and across the top of Fayette County, north of Perry.

Holdover trout can be found well from the mouth of the Cassleman River down to South Connellsville. The Area Manager added that a 27 mile stretch is trout stocked with fingerlings and adults.

Rick Lorson told me that the "Yough" is pronounced YOCK as in dock, so if you are in the area, show off when you go into a tackle store and use that pronunciation. The guy behind the counter may share some secrets with you.

Bill Devine said that the river is his favorite carp spot, flowing north into the Monongahela near McKeesport. He fishes the Fish and Boat Commission launch located just off Route 48 at the Boston Bridge in the town of Boston. Traveling south on State route 51 past Elizabeth, head north on 48 for 7 or 8 miles and you will get to Boston, Pa.

A small park and bicycle trail access area can be found here. Decent sized carp, up to upper teen pounds, are caught by him on canned corn. He really likes to pre-chum his water an hour or two earlier. Bill and I like to kid the guys who don't fish for carp by call-

The Boston Bridge area of the "The Yock" was where
Dave Devine caught and put this 13 pound carp back.

ing them "trash fishermen," and he said that lots of such critters come around to watch what he is doing. When that takes place, he gets in the car and moves away.

Away means heading south on rte 51, turning left onto rte 981 near the I70 intersection, and head south towards Smithton. Before crossing a bridge he turns left (do it carefully, you may think that you are going over a cliff here) where another bicycle path exists. Walk to the river, and fish the calm pool to the left. Chum it up and you will probably be rewarded by a fine catch of carp with perhaps a canoe or two being the only passerbys.

The river gets walleye up in Allegheny County and down through Westmoreland and Fayette Counties.

It has at least 11 boat ramps from top to bottom so you may find that this stretch of water is one that can't be beaten. Then of course, you can head south and fish the lake too!

Northern pike, walleye, trout, large and smallmouth bass, along with panfish are the featured players in this very long lake as it travels from north to south.

Two ramps are found on the Fayette County side, one called Jockey Hollow and the other, Tub Run. Both have ample parking. On the lakes Somerset County shore you will see three more, each with lots of parking. The names are Breast Access, Somerfield North and Somerfield South.

In 1999, Area Manager Lorson said that he expected good catches of 16-19 inch walleye to occur in the lake so you have to know that by now, any that stayed surely are much bigger. And with favorable water, hopefully, many a little 'eye has been born as well.

And now for a few spots that are at least worth mention under the "Honorable" category, try these:

Colver Reservoir — a/k/as Vetera Dam. This 75 acre lake in Cambria County has been stocked since 1996 with walleye, and saugeye.

A good number of largemouth bass were found in a 2000 study with the largest volume of fish by number being white suckers. In cold water, they have firm meat and while nearly impossible to fillet perfectly, a sucker or two might be an alternate to hot dogs one night.

Dutch Fork Lake is a 91 acre site that I read about in a Fisheries Management Field Report too. Located in Donegal Township, Washington County, the lake belongs to Fish and Boat.

Excellent numbers of largemouth bass were sampled and the lake also is trout stocked. Quite a few white crappie are in Dutch Fork and the primary forage fish are gizzard shad. Bullhead and channel catfish are in the lake too, along with saugeye plus muskies-tiger and true-strain's.

Another Honorable Mention lake is Loyalhanna in Westmoreland County. Huge numbers of white and black crappie were captured by a Commission trap netting in 1999 and electrofishing the spring before.

They also found lots of largemouth bass and catfish, with a smattering of muskies of both variations.

And how about the Ohio River? It's sister rivers, The Allegheny And Monagahela are great. Frankly, the Ohio ain't bad either. Call it "Best Spot #51 or 52" or so.

So that about wraps it all up. Pennsylvania, not PITTSBURGH alone, and not even "DIRTY PITTSBURGH" alone.

Once thought of as a Steel Mill that belched smoke into its other cities, The Keystone State has lost that image due to hard work of environmentalists and government — combined with business people too over the last 25 years.

New York isn't just its five boroughs, and New Jersey shouldn't be thought of alone as a place that has too many stinky oil storage sites along it's Turnpike.

Pennsylvania is far more than Pittsburgh and Philadelphia (even though both cities are really nice anyway). The state is huge and its dedicated employees at Fish and Boat are the ones that really should be applauded now — so, from "Gone Fishin'," my personal ATTABOY to all of you!!

Scuze me, gone fishin'
